Advances in Group Work Research

Advances in Group Work Research

Sheldon D. Rose
Aaron M. Brower
Editors

The Haworth Press
New York • London

Advances in Group Work Research has also been published as *Journal of Social Service Research*, Volume 13, Number 2 1989.

The Haworth Press, Inc., 10 Alice Street, Binghamton, NY 13904-1580
EUROSPAN/Haworth, 3 Henrietta Street, London WC2E 8LU England

Library of Congress Cataloging-in-Publication Data

Advances in group work research / Sheldon D. Rose, Aaron M. Brower, editors.
    p. cm.
    "Has also been published as Journal of social service research, volume 13, number 2, 1989"—T.p. verso.
    Includes bibliographical references.
    ISBN 0-86656-983-9
    1. Social group work. I. Rose, Sheldon D. II. Brower, Aaron, M.
HV45.A33   1989
361.4—dc20   89-77595
                                                                CIP

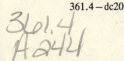

Advances in Group Work Research

CONTENTS

ABOUT THE EDITORS

Sheldon D. Rose, PhD, is Professor of Social Work and Director of the Interpersonal Skills Training and Research Project at the University of Wisconsin at Madison. He has carried out extensive research on the effectiveness of various group approaches for the treatment of children and of adults. In addition to numerous articles, he has written or edited six books on this topic: *Treating Children in Groups: A Behavioral Approach* (1972), *Group Therapy: A Behavioral Approach* (1977), *A Casebook in Group Therapy* (1980), *Working with Children and Adolescents in Groups* (1987), *Research in Group Work* (Haworth Press, 1987), and *Working with Adults in Groups* (1989). He is a coauthor of several manuals for group leaders on topics that include stress management, pain management, and assertiveness training. In addition, he serves as editor of the newsletter, *Empirical Group Work* and as an editorial board member of many social work and psychology journals.

Aaron M. Brower, PhD, is Assistant Professor of Social Work at the University of Wisconsin-Madison and Program Coordinator for the university's Center for New Student Development. In addition to a number of publications in the area of empirical group work practice, research, and theory, he has published widely in the areas of computer utilization and personality psychology. His current research focuses on social-cognitive examinations of stress-and-coping and treatment processes, on how college students make the transition from adolescence to adulthood, and on the development and evaluation of small group programs to assist new students in their transition to university life. Dr. Brower has recently been appointed Associate Editor for the journal, *Small Group Research*.

Advances in Group
Work Research

The Group Work Research Dilemma

Aaron M. Brower
Sheldon D. Rose

SUMMARY. To engage in group treatment research is to find one-self confronting problems inherent to group functioning. These problems are first identified and then illustrated through a discussion of how the authors in this volume grapple with them. It is argued that instead of either oversimplifying group functioning in service of attempting to side-step these research problems, or abandoning group research altogether, practical knowledge about groups can be gained by carefully reviewing how different researchers address these problems, and viewing their results within the context of a developing body of group treatment research.

Research on groups was exploding in the 1950s and 1960s. One could hardly pick up a professional journal of that time without it containing at least a handful of articles about group processes, group outcomes, or group influences on individual behavior. Anthologies of research on group dynamics abounded. Since that fertile time, in spite of the fact that much of current treatment takes place *in* groups, research *about* groups and group processes has been scarce indeed.

This is not to suggest that group research has been abandoned entirely. A number of journals remain devoted to publishing research on group process and group practice, and professional organizations exist for the purpose of bringing together group practitioners. At the same time, the excitement over engaging in group research has waned, and the field itself has become splintered ac-

Aaron M. Brower, PhD, is Assistant Professor and Sheldon D. Rose, PhD, is Professor, School of Social Work, 425 Henry Mall, Madison, WI 53706. Address correspondence to Dr. Brower.

1

cording to professional affiliations and along "practitioner vs. researcher" lines.

The research that is done on groups, too, has most often become either overly simplistic or excessively technological. One explanation for why many social scientists have turned away from doing research on groups is that they inevitably find themselves confronting problems of conceptualization, design, and analysis inherent to the complexity of group functioning and group life. Group research and particularly group treatment research, place an extra layer of problems onto practice research (see Barlow, Hayes & Nelson, 1984, for a review of the problems that beset treatment research).

Recently, an annual series of meetings, the Symposium on Empirical Foundations of Group Work, has provided a forum in which group research issues can be explored. The articles in this volume represent a sample of papers presented at the last three years of these symposia. This is the second volume in what may become a long series. (See Rose and Feldman [1987] for the first in this series.)

The articles in this volume present to the reader a sampling of how different social scientists grapple with the major problems associated with doing research on treatment groups. As is the inherent nature of group research, each decision made by the authors solves some methodological and analytical problems while creating others.

One common problem for group researchers, for example, arises in utilizing control group designs that call for random assignment of subjects into experimental and control conditions. Common to all treatment researchers, group researchers are confronted with the expense of increasing sample sizes and the ethical issues involved in withholding treatment from subjects, yet these problems are compounded by the additional difficulty when a specific type of group composition is desired. Often the researcher, for example, wishes to balance groups with specific proportions of men and women, blacks and whites, or people of different ages. In this event, a stratified approach to sampling and condition assignment is required. This adds exponentially to the required subject pool, and increases threats to non-comparability of conditions.

Another design problem for group researchers is based on the difficulty of applying multivariate methods to practice research even when a large number of uncontrolled variables exist. It is evident that many variables do not have the same impact in one situation as in another. An intervention will have different effects on groups composed of men as compared to women (Garvin & Reed, 1983), when delivered by a male as compared to a female (Brower et al., 1987), when delivered in a long-term insight oriented therapy group vs. a short-term education group (Feldman et al., 1983), or when offered at one stage of group development as compared to another (Feld & Radin, 1982).

Members in a group are likely to be influenced uniquely by the same group conditions. These differences may be further affected by many individual attributes such as age, sex, cognitions, affects or previous group experiences. They may also be affected by the way other members interact with the member in question in terms of his or her role in the group. This raises the further complication relating to whether the unit of analysis will be the individual group member or the group itself (Glisson, 1987). Is a group phenomenon captured simply by averaging member behavior? Is another measure of central tendency a better indicator of group behavior? If member behaviors are aggregated to summarize group phenomena, will the sample size become so small that statistics applied will no longer be sufficiently powerful to discriminate effects? These questions are endemic to group research.

Thus, it is often the case that group work research design decisions force the investigator either to take liberties with the scientific method, or compromise his or her views of the intricacies of group functioning. It is no wonder that when faced with the likelihood of a flawed design, social scientists have moved away from researching groups to other more straightforward research domains.

Ideally, research designs should require the measurement of relevant individual attributes, individual-group interactions, group conditions, leader attributes, and leader interventions. Data analyses should incorporate ways of examining the interactions among these sets of variables. What is more likely is that cost factors require the research to limit a study to only one (or a few) of these variables. The external validity of these findings to other group situations is then limited.

The primary implication of this discussion is the need to develop *programs* of research that systematically vary the many conditions that contribute to outcomes in groups. We need strategies to standardize reporting of results to allow for easier compilations across individual studies. And we need research and analysis designs that can handle complex interactions of group variables, interactions that are not simply artifacts of the ways we analyze the data.

The Symposium on Empirical Foundations of Group Work is committed to addressing the issues mentioned above. Towards this end, the articles appearing in this volume explore many of these concerns. Each article illustrates the decisions and compromises that each researcher must make to explore group phenomenon and treatment. Taken as a set, these articles demonstrate that the old saying that "the whole is greater than the sum of its parts" is particularly true in the field of group research: as a set, these articles complement one another's strengths and weaknesses, and present to us an overall picture of the state-of-the-art in the field of group research. The whole of this volume will hopefully guide the group researcher and practitioner to view the "big picture" of empirical group practice.

The article by Bell, Charping and Strecker illustrates the place that most group research begins, that is, attempting to define the phenomenon of interest that has been observed under the treatment condition (in this case, observed in self-help groups). In their study of groups for recently divorced individuals, their initial question was one of consumer satisfaction: what was it about the group experience that made it a valuable one for the participants? The advantages of their approach were to allow them to increase sample size by aggregating across groups, and to obtain data concerning long-term follow up. The primary disadvantages arise for the exact same things: there are inherent problems in retrospective samples, and once groups are aggregated, any comparison of group conditions is lost. The problems and benefits of such an approach are discussed fully by these authors, recommending to us its use as a jumping off point when beginning a program of research on a new topic.

One logical next step, after defining the phenomenon of interest through the above consumer approach, is to design a comparison group project. The article by Tolman and Bhosley illustrates one classic group research design: the "individual-within-the-group" design (Brower & Garvin, in press), where individual treatment outcomes are investigated within the group context. Tolman and Bhosley use a quasi-experimental design that takes advantage of a relatively large sample and unobtrusive measures. Yet the design strengths lead to the weaknesses of the findings. While the sample size was substantial, the non-random design does not address the threat to validity of non-comparability of treatment conditions.

One solution would have been to use a true experimental design. An example of such a design is found in the article by Tolman and Rose. They compare stress management groups that employ cognitive-behavioral elements along with relaxation techniques, with a treatment consisting of relaxation alone. Both of these treatments are then compared to a wait-list control condition. Randomization is used to assign subjects to conditions, experienced leaders were used, and extensive training was done to assure that leaders were in fact applying the treatment that they were supposed to within each condition. While the use of two comparisons broadens the possibility of generalization, and randomization addresses the non-comparability issue, the expense of doing so precludes using enough participants to obtain adequate power for the analyses. Thus, the main finding that the stress management and relaxation conditions, while both better than the wait-list control condition, did not differ from one another may in fact have been a problem of insufficient statistical power.

Both Tolman and Bhosley and Tolman and Rose discuss these shortcomings in the distinctions they draw between clinical and statistical significance found in their results. A problem not discussed, however, is that while one primary treatment condition was manipulated and therefore explored, the "individual-within-the-group" design does not allow for the manipulation of the effects of group conditions on treatment outcomes.

The article by Kirkham and Schilling can be seen as one approach to make the design of these previous two articles more sophisticated. Efforts were made to raise the sample size while retaining randomization of subjects into conditions. Thus, instead of using primarily bivariate statistics, multivariate statistics could be used. The sample size allowed for adequate power in the analyses, yet in spite of the relatively large sample, the design again, did not allow for manipulation of the effect on outcome of group condition. However, the biggest problem inherent to this study is its monetary and energy expenses; it can only be carried out by the few researchers with major grants or other large sources of funding.

The last two articles in this volume take another approach to the problems identified above. The article by Whitney and Rose was designed specifically to investigate the effects of a group condition on outcome. One condition, namely intensity of member-member communication, was identified as critical to individual change, and was systematically manipulated across the treatment conditions in the stress management packages given to the participants in the study. The problems of power and inadequate sample size again create problems for interpreting these results. Because of the primary research question to explore the effects of group condition on outcome, subjects needed to be spread across four treatment conditions. Subsequently, the cell size within each condition remained too small to rule out extraneous effects, such as those due to group attrition.

In the final article, Flowers and Booarem explore the issue of comparison groups in group research, and develop an alternative strategy. In a series of studies that they conducted, a unique variation of a single-case method was employed whereby members served as their own controls. For each member, two target problems were solicited from members in group treatment, and then only one of them was discussed in group. While cautioning users to the limitations inherent to single-subject designs (see Hayes, 1984), Flowers and Booarem found that their comparison problem method could serve as a viable substitute for a comparison group approach, when expense was an issue.

In all of the articles in this volume, the researchers have struck compromises between the various demands of conducting good research. In each case, the authors selected strategies that strengthened their results in some areas with recognition of the pitfalls of their decisions. As has been demonstrated, research on groups presents a series of dilemmas, to which each researcher must find original solutions. No one study is without imperfection. Yet the inability to design and carry out the perfect study should not deter researchers from carrying out a range of interesting and useful studies which each contribute to a developing body of knowledge on group work and group therapy.

REFERENCES

Barlow, D.H., Hayes, S.C. & Nelson, R.O. (1984) *The scientist practitioner: Research and accountability in clinical and educational settings*. NY: Pergamon.

Brower, A.M. & Garvin, C.D. (1989) Design issues in social group work research. *Social work with groups, 12(3)*, 91-102.

Brower, A.M., Garvin, C.D., Hobson, J., Reed, B.G. & Reed, H. (1987) Exploring the effects of leader gender and race on group behavior. In J. Lassner, K. Powell & E. Finnegan (Eds.), *Social group work. Competence and values in practice*. NY: The Haworth Press, pp. 129-48.

Feld, S. & Radin, N. (1982) *Social psychology for social work and the mental health professions*. NY: Columbia University Press.

Feldman, R.A., Caplinger, T.E. & Wodarski, J.S. (1983) *The St. Louis conundrum: The effective treatment of antisocial youths*. Englewood Cliffs, NJ: Prentice-Hall.

Garvin, C.D. & Reed, B.G. (1983) *Group work with women/group work with men*. NY: The Haworth Press.

Glisson, C. (1987) The group versus the individual as the unit of analysis in small group research. In Rose, S.D. & Feldman, R. (Eds.), *Research Methodology. Applications in Group Work*. NY: The Haworth Press, 15-30.

Hayes, S.C. (1981) Single-case experimental design and empirical clinical practice. *Journal of Consulting and Clinical Psychology, 49(2)*, 193-211.

Rose, S.D. & Feldman, R. (Eds.) (1987). *Research Methodology. Applications in Group Work*. NY: The Haworth Press.

Client Perceptions of the Effectiveness of Divorce Adjustment Groups

William J. Bell
John W. Charping
Jean B. Strecker

SUMMARY. A follow-up study assessing client perceptions of factors which influence the effectiveness of short-term divorce adjustment groups is described. A self-selected sample of 65 participants from twenty-one groups spanning seven years completed an author-designed questionnaire. The findings are reviewed from the perspective of the supportive, therapeutic, and after-group adjustment value of the group experience. The strengths and limitations of a retrospective study design are discussed.

Recently, several descriptive reports on the use of short-term groups for helping clients adjust to divorce have been published (Bonkowski & Wanner-Westly, 1979; Coche & Goldman, 1979; Faust, 1987; Granvold & Welch, 1977, 1979; Morris & Prescott, 1975; Shelton & Nix, 1979; Stephenson & Boler, 1981; Taylor, 1980; and Welch & Granvold, 1977). These authors have suggested that short-term groups can provide: (a) a context to help "normalize" the crazy times most clients experience as they deal with this transitional problem-in-living, (b) a temporary reference group for self-assessment and self-understanding, (c) a source of emotional support at a time when many suffer the loss of family and friends, and (d) an educational experience where information about areas such as parenting, legal matters, and adjustment to a single life can

---

William J. Bell, PhD, and John W. Charping, PhD, are Associate Professors, University of Tennessee, Knoxville, College of Social Work, Nashville Branch, Nashville, TN. Jean B. Strecker, PhD, is Director, Families in Transition Program, Family and Children's Service, Nashville, TN.

be shared and discussed. In each of the programs described, the author presents practice experiences as support for the use of short-term group approach.

Few research studies exist, however, to support the efficacy of this approach to helping divorcing clients. In a study conducted by Kessler (1978), three divorce groups were compared: (a) a structured group in which one-half of the group's time was spent in spontaneous group discussion and the other half on specific skill development exercises, (b) an unstructured group in which the leader responded to participants' needs as they arose, and (c) a "waiting list" control group. Each of the treatment groups met for an eight-hour session followed by eight weekly two-hour sessions. Findings indicated that members in both the structured and the unstructured groups were more successful than control group members in attaining a sense of confidence, emotional autonomy, and self-mastery. Members participating in the structured group also finished with significantly higher levels of positive self-identity and greater self-acceptance than those in the unstructured and control groups.

A study using similar contrast conditions was conducted by Salts and Zongker (1983), though both treatment groups met over a ten-week period with two-and-one-half to three-hour weekly sessions. This study assessed which of the three group conditions would most effectively help ease the transition into single life as measured by improvement in self-concept and post-divorce adjustment. Only those who participated in the structured treatment condition had significantly higher post-divorce adjustment scores than those in the control group. All study participants, however, including those in the control group, had higher self-concept and post-divorce adjustment scores at the end of the group period suggesting that time may be an important healing influence.

Fisher (1976) found that a ten-week group experience of three hours per week focused on helping members work through the divorcing process significantly improved the experimental group participants' adjustment in the following areas: (a) self-acceptance of divorce, (b) disentanglement of the love relationship, (c) rebuilding social relationships, (d) total divorce adjustment, and (e) improved self-concept. Gillen (1976), used paraprofessionals to lead four two-and-one-half-hour weekly sessions for separated or divorced persons. Using a post-test only control group research design, Gillen found no significant difference in the effects on participants' self-concepts between the treatment and the control groups. In a structured nine-week group reported by Reid (1978), the treatment condition group showed a reduction in feelings of alienation while the non-treatment group showed no change. Neither group showed significant change in feelings of social isolation, powerlessness, and normlessness. In summary, while there is some evidence to indicate that short-term treatment groups can be helpful to clients in some areas of divorce adjustment such as in self-acceptance and overall divorce adjustment where similar improvement was obtained in two studies; in other areas such as improved self-concept, self-identity, self-mastery, and self-autonomy, the evidence is limited to the findings of one study or, as in the case of improved self-concept, contradictory. Equally unclear in the research is evidence about the kind of group conditions that facilitate client growth or change.

One way to gain further information about the effects of a treatment approach as well as the group conditions that fostered these effects is through the use of a post-group questionnaire in which client perceptions of their experience are systematically assessed. While such information can not be used as evidence to support the efficacy of a treatment approach, client perceptions of their experience can be a valuable aid to enhancing or modifying particular interventive strategies as well as supplying important information about which aspects of the group experience would be fertile ground for future research (Bloom, Hodges, Kern, & McFaddin, 1985; Yalom, 1985). Considering (a) the current state of knowledge about the use of short-term groups with divorcing clients, (b) the potential information that could be obtained from such a study, and (c) the availability of a large pool of clients who had attended short-term divorce adjustment groups, a follow-up study was conducted to assess client perceptions of the factors which influence the effectiveness of short-term groups in assisting them in their adjustment to divorce.

METHOD

Group Program

The group program consisted of a combination of structured and unstructured group experiences designed to make possible the development of a therapeutic support group. The following group format was used during the entire period covered by this study (Charping, Bell, & Strecker).[1] The first group session was used to set the stage for what was to follow. A contract was established and all members had an opportunity to tell the group about their divorcing experience, what they wanted to get from the group, and what areas they wanted discussed. The second session was primarily used to present and discuss the stages of the divorcing process. While sessions three through nine allowed for a good deal of flexibility in areas of discussion, each session began with participants sharing what their week had been like; their successes and problems. From these and other areas suggested at the first session, topics for discussion evolved. To facilitate and enhance these discussions, various group exercises and outside assignments were used. The particular exercise or assignment used varied depending on individual and group needs. In the final session, members reviewed their progress: where they were at the beginning of the group, where they were at the end, and what they wanted and needed to work on after the group. Each member was also given feedback from the rest of the group on their perceptions of the member's progress and future work.

Participants for the groups were actively recruited from within the agency clientele and outside the agency using the media and professional referrals. A social worker screened all potential participants. Only persons who were divorced or had separated and filed for divorce were admitted to the groups. The typical group was three-fourths female and one-fourth male. Groups met for ten sessions, each an hour-and-one-half long. All groups were co-led by a male and a female masters-level social worker.

---

1. For further details on the divorce adjustment program, see Charping, J. W., Bell, W. J., & Strecker, J. B. Short-term group treatment for adjustment to divorce. Unpublished manuscript, University of Tennessee at Nashville, 1988.

Sample Population

A total of 212 clients participated in twenty-one divorce adjustment groups held at Family and Children's Service in Nashville, Tennessee over the seven year period covered by this study. Current addresses were located for 137. Three of these participants helped in the development of the post-group questionnaire used in the study. Thus, the study population was 134. Fifty-one percent or 68 clients responded to the questionnaire. Sixty-five of these were usable as the sample population. The results of the study are based on the responses of a self-selected sample of 65 persons from the study population of 134 persons.

Seventy-seven percent of the sample ($n = 65$) were at the time of the group experience between the age of 30 and 40 with 12 percent below and 11 percent above 40 years of age. Twenty-eight percent were male and 71 percent female. Seventy-seven percent had been married once; 23 percent, twice. Forty-six percent of the participants were divorced at the time they attended the group. The remainder had filed for divorce and were divorced sometime during or soon after the group. Eighty-nine percent had children, and of this group, 61 percent had sole or joint custody; 29 percent had adult children.

Comparison of Sample with the Study Population

The sample ($n = 65$) was similar to the study population (N $= 134$) in all areas where data was available for most of study population: age (t $= 1.48$, df $= 192$, p $= .14$), sex (t $= -.99$, df $= 197$, p $= .32$), length of marriage (t $= .89$, df $= 197$, p $= .37$), employment (t $= .55$, df $= 197$, p $= .58$), the percentage with children (t $= .11$, df $= 197$, p $= .91$), and the number of sessions attended (t $= .86$, df 161, p $= .39$).

Questionnaire

The author-designed questionnaire was constructed with the following assessment questions in mind: (1) What aspects of the group experience were viewed as helpful or not helpful? (2) Did the respondents view the group experience as having any lasting effects and, if so, what were they? (3) What aspects of the group program were experienced as helpful? (4) What characteristics of the client or the client's situation may have influenced his/her perceptions of the group experience? In each section of the questionnaire, the authors focused their attention on developing items that would take into account: previous research findings, areas of interest suggested in articles describing short-term divorce adjustment treatment groups, and the stated purposes of the divorce adjustment groups under study.

The questionnaire developed took approximately 20 to 30 minutes to complete. The first section consisted of 25 questions which explored the respondents' experience while attending the group (e.g., "I learned more about myself through hearing others talk about their problems," "I felt I was accepted by other members," "The group experience helped me feel better about myself"). Respondents were given a five-point Likert-type scale (strongly agree, agree, no opinion, disagree, strongly disagree) to indicate the response level that best reflected their assessment of which group forces or factors were most therapeutic or helpful. Many of the items used in this section represented an adaptation of the items developed by Yalom (1985) in his retrospective study on curative factors in treatment groups. A second section of the questionnaire dealt with the degree to which participants felt the group experience had helped them deal with problems *after* the group was over (e.g., feelings of self-worth, anger, developing new relationships). A five-point Likert-type scale was used (helped greatly, helped some, not a concern, and made worse). This section contained many items developed by Bloom (1985) in his longitudinal study of persons going through the divorce process. Participants were asked to evaluate aspects of the group program in the third section (e.g., number and length of sessions, degree of structure, presence of male/female leaders). In the final section demographic information such as sex, age, marital status, and employment were solicited. Open-ended questions were added to the first three sections to allow participants the opportunity to provide information about their experience not covered in closed response items.

A pre-test of the questionnaire was conducted using three former group members each representing a different group and a different time period (1980, 1983, and 1985). After completing the questionnaire, each pre-test respondent was interviewed resulting in appropriate adjustments to the questionnaire.

Study Procedure

All former group participants who had attended one or more sessions and for whom a current address could be located (134) received a letter introducing the purpose of the study, a form giving the researchers permission to use their questionnaire, a copy of the questionnaire, and two stamped, self-addressed envelopes. One of the self-addressed envelopes was to be used to return the completed questionnaire, the other to return the permission form. Since no name was requested on the questionnaire, this procedure assured respondent anonymity and provided the researchers with a way to keep track of those who returned their questionnaires. Two follow-up letters were mailed; one two weeks after the original mailing, the second four weeks later.

RESULTS AND DISCUSSION

More than 95 percent of the study sample reported that they had found the short-term group experience helpful or very helpful overall. The two areas of helpfulness most frequently reflected throughout the data were (a) the opportunity to be with other people who were going through a similar experience (supportive value) and (b) the opportunity to gain a better understanding of themselves and their situations (therapeutic value). To facilitate the analysis in these areas, related items were grouped into categories based on Yalom's (1985) work on curative factors in treatment groups and on the intended use of a particular item as developed by the researchers. In addition to these findings, data are presented on client perceptions related to the "after effects" of the group experience as well as their reactions to the program format.

Supportive Aspects of Group Experience

As shown in Table 1 by the mean percentage scores for questionnaire items related to "Supportive Benefits" of group, 83 percent of the participants strongly agreed or agreed that their group had been supportive. With one exception, there was a positive relationship between members' perceptions of group support and overall group helpfulness: "Realized other people cared" (Kendall Tau C = .156, p < .04); "Felt accepted by group members" (Kendall Tau C = .168, p < .05); "Felt group was close" (Kendall Tau C = .265, p < .03); and "Felt part of group closeness" (Kendall Tau C = .283, p < .01). The item, "Felt accepted by group leaders," was not significantly related (Kendall Tau C = .106, p < .11).

Group participants were encouraged to have contact with each other outside the group. Sixty-four percent took advantage of this source of support by having contact with one another up to five times a week. As indicated in open-ended responses, for many group participants these "during group associations" became the beginning of long-lasting friendships and in some cases a long-lasting support network. Fifty-nine percent indicated that they continued to have contact with other group members after the group was over.

More than eighty percent of the sample strongly agreed or agreed that they had other sources of support while attending the group. Forty-one percent listed their friends as supportive and 32 percent listed their family. While almost 60 percent of the participants had seen or were being seen by counselors at the time of the group experience, less than 17 percent listed their counselors as a source of support. Church as a source of support was identified even less frequently (4%) although 63 percent indicated that they were active to moderately active in a church at the time.

In summary, the majority of the sample population used the group as a support system even though most had other available sources of support. This finding represents somewhat of a challenge to the assertion made by several authors that one of the major reasons divorcing persons come to groups is because they have lost

Table 1

Percentage of Responses by
Supportive Benefits of Group Experience[a]

Supportive Benefits	Strongly Agree	Agree	No Opinion	Disagree	Strongly Disagree
			Percentage of Responses		
Realized other people cared	29	58	11	2	–
Felt accepted by group members	45	48	6	1	–
Felt accepted by group leaders	58	37	3	2	–
Felt group was close	28	44	16	11	1
Felt part of group closeness	28	42	17	11	2
Mean % of all items	37	46	11	5	1

[a] <u>n</u> = 65 for each

most, if not all, of their support systems. Evidently, the group was viewed by potential members as a viable way to meet this need, but not out of a lack of support systems. Nelson (1980), however, provides a possible explanation for what seems to be an inconsistency in the findings by suggesting that there are several types of support needs (protection, acceptance, validation, and education). A divorce adjustment group may provide one or more of these needs not met by other available sources of support. While such data was not obtained in this study, more specific information about how members use the group as a source of support would be very helpful to practitioners, particularly as they plan service programs for this client population.

Therapeutic Aspects of the Group Experience

The results related to the therapeutic value of the group experience are separated into four areas (each an area of focus in the questionnaire as well as in the group program): learning about self, interpersonal learning, affirmation of self, and instillation of hope.

Learning About Self

As indicated by the first item under the category of "Learning About Self" in Table 2, more than 96 percent of the sample either strongly agreed or agreed that they had gained an increased understanding of what they were going through at the time of the group. Not surprisingly, the more members thought they had learned about their divorce experience, the more helpful they viewed the group experience overall (Kendall's Tau C = .240. p < .01).

Getting in touch with feelings was a major area of self-learning. Ninety percent of the respondents reported that the group helped them get in touch with the feelings they were experiencing. Over fifty different feelings were listed. These were grouped into 20 categories. "Anger" was by far the most frequently identified feeling. It was listed by more than 60 percent of the respondents. "Loneliness" was second, identified by 20 percent of the respondents. Other feelings identified included were "frustration" (19%), "rejection" (17%), "depression" (17%), "fear" (15%), "guilt"

(15%), positive feelings about self (13%), grief (11%), and "negative feelings about self" (11%).

The dominance of anger as an identified feeling is similar to results obtained elsewhere such as in a recent follow-up study conducted by Wallerstein (1986). She found that even ten years after divorce, intense anger was still present in many of the parents who participated in her study (40% of the women, close to 30% of the men). The relatively low frequency with which grief, depression, and rejection were mentioned by the participants was unexpected because these emotions were frequently expressed during group sessions. One possible explanation is that anger is an emotion which overlays other emotions such as these and which persists longer as a predominate feeling.

It is difficult to know what meaning to give these findings, however, given the vulnerability of follow-up exploratory studies to retrospective bias explanations. For example, the expression of anger was encouraged by the leaders of the groups as well as in popular literature. The strength of this feeling area, as indicated in the data, may be a reflection of the leaders' practice bias rather than a reality of the members' personal experience. A content/feeling analysis of group sessions would be a helpful way to begin to look at how often anger and other feelings are expressed and dealt with at least within the group.

Self-understanding was a second major area of self-learning. Approximately 75 percent thought they were helped to face, understand, and accept good and bad feelings they had toward themselves. Almost 60 percent reported they had discovered things about themselves they hadn't known before such as: learning about the roles they played in their marriages, how they tended to work on problems, and how they interacted in interpersonal relationships.

The two methods reported as most useful for self-learning included (a) vicarious learning or spectator therapy and (b) direct feedback. Approximately 90 percent reported that they had learned more about themselves through hearing others talk about their own problems. As one member put it: "Hearing others tell about their situation helped me get in touch with what I was feeling and think-

Table 2 (Part I)

Percentage of Responses by
Area of Therapeutic Benefit[a]

Therapeutic Area	Percentage of Responses				
	Strongly Agree	Agree	No Opinion	Disagree	Strongly Disagree
Learning about Self Items					
Increased understanding of my divorcing experience	48	48	3	1	–
Got in touch with feelings	33	57	8	2	–
Accept good feelings about self	20	59	16	5	–
Accept bad feelings about self	11	64	20	5	–
New discoveries about self	20	39	25	16	–
Mean % of all items	26	53	15	6	–

Interpersonal Learning Items

Item					
Feelings and attitudes of others	48	52	-	-	-
Similarity of experience	26	63	11	-	-
Accept bad feelings about ex-spouse	15	72	8	5	-
Accept good feelings about ex-spouse	3	47	32	18	-
More realistic expectations in male/female relationships	10	61	19	10	-
Strengths and weaknesses in male/female relationships	10	47	24	19	-
Relating to opposite sex	6	37	31	26	-
Mean % of all items	26	53	15	6	1

[a] $\underline{n}$ = 65 for each

Table 2 (Part II)

Percentage of Responses by
Area of Therapeutic Benefit[a]

Therapeutic Area	Percentage of Responses				
	Strongly Agree	Agree	No Opinion	Disagree	Strongly Disagree
Affirmation of Self Items					
Accepted by group leaders	58	37	3	2	—
Accepted by group members	45	48	6	1	—
Felt better about self	38	51	6	5	—
Group members cared	29	58	11	2	—
Mean % of all items	42	48	7	3	—
Installation of Hope Item					
Provided sense of hope	33	54	8	2	3

[a] $\underline{n}$ = 65 for each

22

ing." Many of the "most critical group incidents" reported by group members included comments about how they had learned to deal with their problems by hearing how other members had dealt with their's (Yalom).[2]

In terms of direct feedback, approximately 90 percent of the respondents thought they had received helpful feedback about their thoughts and feelings. Somewhat fewer, 75 percent, thought they had received helpful feedback about their behavior.

Examples of the kind of self-learning that occurred were stated as follows: "I made a very sexist statement to another member who told me exactly what she thought of it. That led me to seriously look at a part of me that I really didn't like very well." Another respondent commented ". . . when I said, 'He left me and he had no right to expect my children to spend the holidays with him,' I was jumped on by one of the members about how selfish and self-centered I was. It worked."

Interpersonal Learning

As shown by the first item under "Interpersonal Learning" on Table 2, all respondents (100%) either strongly agreed or agreed that they had learned more about other people's feelings and attitudes through attending the group. Several areas of learning about others are particularly noteworthy:

1. Universal nature of their problem. One of the most valuable pieces of information acquired by most participants (approximately 90%) was the discovery that other group members were having similar reactions to the divorcing process. Typical comments include: ". . . knowing that I was not alone nor the first to have the experience and feelings I was having," or "the best aspect of the group was knowing others were having experiences similar to mine."

2. Male/female relationships. Over 70 percent indicated that they had been helped to develop more realistic expectations in male/female relationships. This was complemented by the finding that over 55 percent thought they had become more aware of their

---

2. For a discussion of "critical incidents" in groups, see Yalom, I. D. *The Theory and Practice of Group Psychotherapy*, (3rd ed.). New York: Basic Books, Inc. Publishers, 1985.

strengths and weaknesses in male/female relationships. One member commented that he became aware of some of his distorted interactions with his ex-spouse by noticing that he was creating the same distorted interactions in the group. Approximately 45 percent of the respondents thought they had learned important information about how they related to members of the opposite sex from participating in the group. As one member put it, "The single most important learning was to find out that there were two sides to divorce: the male and the female and the way each looks at marriage." Over 90 percent of the respondents strongly agreed or agreed that it was helpful to have the perspectives of both the female and male leaders in the group.

3. *Ex-spouse.* More than 85 percent of the respondents reported that they had been helped to face and accept bad feelings about their ex-spouse. This is particularly important since over one-half of the participants felt they had been "dumped" and often thought of themselves as "at fault" for not having done enough in the marriage.

Affirmation of Self

Learning that one is "normal" and can be liked and accepted is a powerful therapeutic force towards self-affirmation that can occur within a supportive group. As indicated in Table 2, the data confirmed that the divorce adjustment group provided this therapeutic force. Approximately 90 percent of the respondents reported that they were helped to feel better about themselves; 93 percent felt accepted by other members; 95 percent felt accepted by the group leaders; and over 85 percent indicated that the group had helped them realize that other people care. The following were typical comments: "to be told that I was a good person," "to know that I was really worth something to somebody," and "feeling self-pity and fear in front of others and having them tell me that this happens to everyone."

Instillation of Hope

Of the total respondents, over 85 percent thought they had gained a sense of hope from the group experience (see Table 2). Responses to open-ended question revealed some of the sources of this hope: (a) Several reported that having members of the group at different stages of the divorcing process was beneficial. As one respondent put it, "It was helpful to know that others have gone through this and have survived." (b) Many respondents indicated that in comparison to others they were much better off than they thought. One client stated that "I saw that other people had much less freedom than I did. My situation was not hopeless!" Another client reported, "It was a comfort to know others are hurting too — some even more than me." (c) Several other respondents indicated that it gave them a sense of hope to learn that there were predictable phases they would go through and that, with time and work, they might gain more personal freedom and identity. As might be expected, respondents who viewed the group as providing a sense of hope also perceived the group as being helpful (Kendall's Tau C = .346, p < .01).

Post-Group Adjustment

Information requested which dealt with the "carry-over" effects of the group experience focused on two areas: (a) dealing with feelings and (b) handling practical concerns such as parenting and legal matters (see Table 3).

Feelings

As indicated by the mean percentage scores of feeling items in Table 3, 80 percent of the participants agreed or strongly agreed that the group experience had helped them to handle better a range of feelings after the group was over. Again, as with feelings dealt with during the group experience, anger was the feeling with which most group members experienced assistance. Ninety percent indicated that the group experience continued to be helpful in dealing with this feeling. Seven other feelings were identified by at least 70 percent of the respondents. These included in descending order: self-worth (86%), isolation (83%), self-blame (79%), anxiety (77%), loneliness (77%), depression (75%), and guilt (74%).

The percentages of respondents who reported the group helped them get in touch with their feelings while attending the group (ranging from 11 to 20 percent except for anger at 60 percent) were

Table 3

Percentage of Responses by
Area of Post-Group Adjustment[a]

| Adjustment Area | Percentage of Responses | | | | |
	Helped Greatly	Helped Some	Not a Concern	Did not Help	Made Worse
Feelings					
Anger	34	56	3	5	2
Self-worth	18	68	8	6	—
Isolation	31	52	8	9	—
Self-blame	20	59	13	8	—
Loneliness	24	53	6	14	3
Anxiety	6	71	6	14	3
Depression	20	55	9	14	2
Guilt	19	55	17	9	—
Mean % of all items	21	59	9	10	1

Practical Concerns

Parenting	13	49	18	20	—
Homemaking	5	30	52	13	—
Legal	5	28	52	15	—
Health	3	25	61	11	—
Work Related	5	22	54	19	—
Financial	3	19	52	26	—
Mean % of all items	6	29	48	17	

[a] n = 65 for all items except "Parenting," n = 45

quite different from the percentages of respondents who thought the group experience had helped them deal with feelings after the group ended. Questionnaire design may have contributed to the difference. In the former, the participants were asked to respond to an open-ended question while in the latter the feelings were listed and respondents had only to check the degree to which the group had or had not been helpful with a particular feeling. This difference in question design limited further comparative analysis. In spite of this limitation, however, the data clearly indicated that the majority of the respondents thought they were helped to get in touch with their anger during the group experience and to deal with it more effectively after the group was over.

Practical Concerns

Only 35 percent reported that the group experience had helped them deal with practical concerns such as work-related difficulties, legal problems, financial concerns, and home-making responsibilities (see mean percentage scores under "Practical Concerns" in Table 3). In general the respondents did not view the group as having been a valuable resource in these areas. The one exception to this overall finding was in the area of parenting. Sixty-two percent of the respondents who had children living at home (n = 45) thought the group experience had helped them deal with parenting responsibilities. Particularly for those parents who had children under the age of 21, parenting issues were a major area of discussion for them in almost all groups.

The difference in the degree to which the group experience helped respondents deal with feelings as opposed to practical concerns after the group was over was consistent with how the groups were structured. Although practical concerns were discussed to some degree in all groups, no systematic attention was given to each of the problem areas assessed. In most cases members were encouraged to make use of other available resources to provide assistance in these areas.

Reaction to Group Program and Leaders

Generally, respondents had favorable reactions to the structure and content of the group program. Eighty-five percent reported that they liked the degree of structure used in the group sessions. Length and number of sessions was viewed by the respondents as being "about right," 72% and 60% respectively. However, thirty-five percent indicated a desire for more sessions while twenty-eight thought sessions were too short in length.

With regard to leadership, eighty percent of the respondents reported that group leaders provided the right amount of information, structure, and direction for the group. Over ninety percent preferred having a male and a female leader in the group.

IMPLICATIONS

Upon reflecting on the nature of the findings derived from a retrospective, post-group questionnaire, several concerns or limitations emerge. While the study sample viewed the group experience positively, there was no feasible way to know how the group experience was viewed by approximately 45 percent of the "available client" population that chose not to return the questionnaire. Since no agreement with group members for such a follow-up study had been obtained at the end of each group, the researchers thought that follow-up by mail only for a non-response was least intrusive and the most appropriate.

Another concern centered around the fact that for some of the participants several years had elapsed since they had participated in the group, while for others it have been only a few months. Comments from some of the earlier participants indicated that they could not remember specific details of the group experience especially those related to the group program. They were able to recall, however, their general impressions of the group experience as well as incidents in the group that been particularly meaningful to them. In hindsight, an item in the questionnaire for participants to indicate how well they thought they remembered the group experience would have provided useful information. It is also possible that the response rate may have been affected by "lack of recall" since a larger percentage of members from more recent group members responded to the questionnaire. The response rate may have been improved by asking participants to scan the information sought and providing them an early opportunity to respond to an item such as: "Can't remember enough about the group experience to fill out this questionnaire, but on the whole, I feel positively or negatively about the experience."

Other concerns center around the limitation of a self-report measure and a retrospective study. Two of the more immediate concerns include the following. First, the selection of items to be included in the questionnaire was subject to a selection bias. Even though the selection was guided by stated group objectives, previous research, and "practice wisdom," it is very feasible that critical data was not gathered because the opportunity was not provided in the questionnaire. A second limitation is in the post-hoc nature of the analysis in which one is very susceptible to "seeing what one wants to see" in the data both in how data is analyzed and interpreted.

In spite of these limitations, however, a retrospective study provides a means to obtain feedback from clients in a systematic fashion on the degree to which they valued (or did not value) various aspects of their group experience. This design also minimizes the "gift giving" which can characterize the feedback given on post-group evaluation instruments in the last session. The retrospective design also focuses on those aspects of the group experience that respondents perceive as having lasting effects. In addition, the number of groups and clients sampled is large enough to make possible (a) the assessment of program effectiveness under a variety of group conditions (e.g., composition, size, and leadership), and (b) the use of more sophisticated analysis of the data.

Given these strengths and limitations, it seems appropriate to view the present study as a beginning road map for future research rather than a statement of what really is or is not helpful to clients facing divorce. With this in mind, the following are recommended as fruitful areas for future research: (a) Since identifying and learning how to deal with feelings was consistently perceived as one of the most helpful aspects of the group experience, a more careful "monitoring" and pre-post-group measurement of this process should be considered. Research in this area should be designed to identify those procedures most effective in helping clients learn how to identify and productively manage their feelings; (b) Regarding the supportive aspects of the group experience, more careful assessment of both the clients' reasons for joining and their social situation upon entering the group would provide valuable information about who benefits most from this type of short-term group experience, the type of support most needed, and the time during the divorcing process at which a group is most beneficial; (c) Finally, a pre-post, delayed-post-group assessment of a participant's self-knowledge and self-understanding would help identify and more clearly define the ways in which the group assists members with various aspects of their adjustment.

CONCLUSION

The findings from this study support the assertions made in the literature that short-term groups provide a helpful experience for clients struggling with adjustment to divorce. Participants viewed the group experience as a valuable source of support; a means for identifying, understanding, and accepting feelings about themselves and others; and a means to regain self-respect and hope for the future. Hopefully, this exploratory research will lay the groundwork for further research designed to identify aspects of group treatment that are most beneficial to persons facing this transitional, stressful problem-in-living.

REFERENCES

Bloom, B. L., Hodges, W. F., Kern, M. B., & McFaddin, S. C. A preventive intervention program for the newly separated: Final evaluations. *American Journal of Orthopsychiatry* 1985, 55 (1), 9-26.

Bonkowski, S. E. & Wanner-Westly, B. The divorce group: A new treatment modality. *Social Casework* 1979, 60 (9), 552-57.

Coche, J. & Goldman, J. Brief group psychotherapy for women after divorce: Planning a focused experience. *Journal of Divorce*, 1979, 3 (2), 153-160.

Faust, R. G. A model of divorce adjustment for use in family service agencies. *Social Work*, 1987, 32 (1), 78-80.

Fisher, B. F. Identifying and meeting needs of formerly-married people through a divorce adjustment seminar. (Doctoral dissertation, University of Northern Colorado, 1976), *Dissertation Abstracts International*, 1976, 37, 7036A, (University Microfilms No. 77-11,057,104).

Gillen, F. C. A study of the effects of paraprofessionally conducted group therapy on the self concept of divorced or separated persons. (Doctoral dissertation,

University of South Dakota, 1976), *Dissertation Abstracts International*, 1976, *37* 4883A, (University Microfilms No. 77-3443,74).

Granvold, D. K. & Welch, G. J. Intervention for postdivorce adjustment problems: The treatment seminar. *Journal of Divorce*, 1977, 1 (1), 81-92.

Granvold, D. K. & Welch, G. J. Structured, short-term group treatment of post-divorce adjustment. *International Journal of Group Psychotherapy*, 1979, 29 (3), 347-358.

Keesler, S. Building skills in divorce adjustment groups. *Journal of Divorce*, 1978, 2 (2), 209-216.

Morris, J. D. & Prescott, M. R. Transition groups: An approach to dealing with post-partnership anguish. *The Family Coordinator*, 1975, 24 (3), 325-330.

Nelson, J. C. Support: A necessary condition for change. *Social Work*, 1980, 25 (5), 388-92.

Reid, V. L. The influence of group counseling on the recently divorced. (Doctoral dissertation, Oklahoma State University, 1978), *Dissertation Abstracts International*, 1978, 39, 4737A, (University Microfilms No. 7903731,123).

Salts, C. J. & Zongker, C. E. Effects of divorce counseling groups on adjustment and self concept. *Journal of Divorce*, 1983, 6 (4), 55-67.

Shelton, S. C. & Nix, C. Development of a divorce adjustment group program in a social service agency. *Social Casework*, 1979, 60 (5), 309-312.

Stephenson, S. J. & Boler, M. F. Group treatment for divorcing persons. *Social Work with Groups*, 1981, 4 (3/4), 67-77.

Taylor, J. W. Using short-term structured groups with divorce clients. *Social Casework*, 1980, 61 (7), 433-437.

Wallerstein, J. S. Women after divorce: Preliminary report from a ten-year follow-up. *American Journal of Orthopsychiatry*, 1986, 56 (1), 65-77.

Welch, G. J. & Granvold, D. K. Seminars for separated/divorced: An educational approach to post-divorce adjustment. *Journal of Sex and Marital Therapy*, 1977, 3 (1), 31-39.

Yalom, I. D. *The Theory and Practice of Group Psychotherapy*, (3rd ed.). New York: Basic Books, Inc., Publishers, 1985.

A Comparison of Two Types of Pregroup Preparation for Men Who Batter

Richard M. Tolman
Gauri Bhosley

SUMMARY. This article describes a comparison of the efficacy of two pregroup preparation formats for reducing drop-outs from groups for men who batter their female partners. Eighty men attending a weekly, four-session preparation group were compared with 103 men attending an intensive eight hour workshop format prior to joining open-ended, ongoing groups. The quasi-experimental comparison revealed that the intensive workshop format resulted in significantly fewer drop-outs from the ongoing group prior to completion of four sessions.

A growing awareness of the plight of battered women in the past decade, due largely to the efforts of the battered women's movement, has created widespread services and shelter for battered women and children (Schecter, 1983). More recently, men who batter have also become the focus of treatment services. The advocates for treatment of men who batter believe that such services have a legitimate and

Richard M. Tolman, PhD, is Assistant Professor at Jane Addams College of Social Work and is Research Coordinator, Crisis Center for South Suburbia. Gauri Bhosley, MSW, is Associate Research Coordinator, Crisis Center for South Suburbia.

A previous version of this paper was presented at the Third Symposium for the Empirical Foundations of Group Work, Chicago, IL, May 15-18, 1987.

This study was supported by a grant from the Sophia Fund, Chicago, IL. The authors wish to gratefully acknowledge Pat Anderson, Terry Ann Andersen, Kathy Blaszkiewicz, John Dietche, Christine Mendoza, Marianne Piet, and Harrison Williams for their work in developing and implementing the pregroup preparation formats, and for their assistance at all phases of the research process.

important place in the effort to eradicate domestic violence (Gondolf, 1987).

Men who batter enter treatment, for the most part, because they are court-mandated or wife-mandated (i.e. their wives or partners have left or have threatened to leave the relationship). Their primary motive is rarely to stop the abuse itself but rather to placate the courts or their wives. They are likely to drop out of treatment if their partners return, if they are convinced their partners will not return despite their efforts in treatment, or if they are not convinced of the willingness of the court to follow-through with negative sanctions.

Treatment for men who batter generally takes place in the form of group sessions (Myers and Eddy, 1984). The high drop-out rate common in these treatment groups suggests the need to develop interventions aimed at reducing drop-outs (Deschner and O'Neil, 1985; Brekke, 1987). This study describes an evaluation of the impact of an intensive pregroup preparation workshop designed to decrease the drop-out rate in these groups.

Many authors have called for greater practitioner involvement in research in social work (Bloom and Fischer, 1982), and specifically in social work groups (Anderson, 1987). In order for such involvement to occur, barriers to research in applied settings must be removed, and a balance struck between service needs and research demands. For example, it is quite difficult to carry out true experimental research in applied settings. Time-consuming or intrusive data-gathering presents another barrier to research in social work agencies. Among the many solutions suggested for bridging the practice-research gap in social work are the use of quasi-experimental designs, and unobtrusive measurement techniques (Anderson, 1987; Bloom and Fischer, 1982). This paper describes the application a quasi-experimental design, with unobtrusive data collection, to add empirical support for the use of a clinical group technique.

MODELS OF PREGROUP PREPARATION
FOR MEN WHO BATTER

Brekke (1987) developed a model for group preparation of men who batter with the following goals: (1) building cohesion; (2) introducing the group members to behavioral techniques; (3) providing group members with a non-judgmental setting to allow them to express their feelings and thoughts about the violent incidents and about entering treatment; (4) educating the group members and confronting them on their behavior; (5) introducing group members to the rationale, techniques, and treatment model of the structured skills group. Brekke studied one six-session orientation group, with 12 members attending at least one group. The results of the study indicate that high levels of cohesion were reached during the orientation group sessions. There was a relatively low drop-out rate for the orientation group itself, 25%. Of the men who joined the structured cognitive-behavioral group following orientation, only one dropped out. He concluded that the orientation group was successful in engaging and preparing the men for subsequent group treatment.

Deschner and O'Neil (1984) developed a one-day intensive workshop to reduce the drop-out rate in their treatment group of wife abusers and child abusers. Without the workshop, 57% of the clients completed 4 or more sessions (of the total 8 sessions). There was an 80% completion rate for those who attended the workshop. Statistical analysis of this single-system study indicated that the increase in completion rate was statistically significant.

Several factors limit generalizations of Deschner and O'Neil's study to groups for men who batter their partners. It was noted that a higher percentage of child abusers remained in counseling for at least 4 sessions. Therefore, the drop-out rate for men who batter their partners was higher than the total percentage reported. Their study included both the victim and the abuser in the treatment. This creates a different context for treatment than male-only treatment. In addition, the differential drop-out rate for men and women was not reported.

This study attempted to assess the relative efficacy of these two types of pregroup preparation for men who batter: weekly and intensive workshop format. The study examined men's groups sponsored by a shelter for battered women. The program initially used a weekly session format for group preparation. Staff subsequently developed an intensive workshop format for pre-group preparation. This created an opportunity to compare the drop-out rates of clients who attended weekly pregroup sessions, and clients who attended the intensive weekend workshop.

PROGRAM DESCRIPTION

The current study was undertaken at the Crisis Center for South Suburbia, an agency in the Chicago area serving battered women, men who batter, and their children. The agency's philosophy played an integral part in the development of the program for men who batter. The agency places the responsibility of the violent incident on the abuser. Conjoint therapy is not advocated until the abuser has taken responsibility for the violence, stopped the violence for several months, and both the victim and abuser are willing to begin conjoint work. Men must first learn to stop the violent behavior and learn alternative skills for coping with emotional arousal and for conflict resolution before beginning any couple's treatment.

The service system for men who batter operates as follows. The abuser must call the agency himself to initiate treatment. The two subsequent individual intake sessions focus on obtaining demographic material and clinical information, and engaging the client in the treatment process. The client is assessed for suitability (clients with untreated substance abuse problems or more than moderate psychopathology are generally not accepted in the program). The abuser is then required to sign both a non-violence pledge and a statement accepting the fact that the agency will be conducting violence checks (i.e. contacting his partner bi-monthly to ascertain the level of violence in the relationship). Given successful completion of the intake process, the man will then begin pregroup preparation, and subsequently an ongoing, open-membership group.

METHOD

Subjects

All of the 183 clients who attended group preparation sessions from 1/1/85 to 12/31/86 were included in the study. All the group members were male, and they were wife abusers. The group members were 85% white, with 7.5% hispanic and 7.5% black. Their ages ranged from 20 to 63. The average age was 35. Thirty-nine percent were court-ordered or court-recommended into treatment.

Design

As previously mentioned, the comparison groups consisted of 1 year of pregroup members and 1 year of orientation workshop members. Therefore, clients were not randomly assigned to the groups. Each pregroup format was studied for a full year to eliminate the confound of seasonal differences.

Measures

The dependent measure in the study is the number of sessions each participant attended while enrolled in the program. Attendance data were gathered session by session by group leaders and systematically reported to the program's clinical director.

The demographic data reported were gathered in standardized intake sessions.

Weekly Pregroup Format

The weekly pregroup format consisted of an open group with a maximum of four group sessions. The purpose of the weekly pregroup was to provide a supportive environment for the group members. It allowed the group members to do some "storytelling" and to vent their frustrations and the anger that they felt toward their wives and the legal system. In order to avoid building resistance to treatment, their feelings were acknowledged but not confronted at this time.

The weekly format also contained some techniques for controlling the violence. The men were taught to take time outs. The men were encouraged to tell their partners about this technique in order to gain their cooperation. This technique involves taking responsibility for one's own actions usually by leaving the situation before it escalated into a violent incident. In the pregroup sessions, the men learned to recognize physical cues that signal tension (e.g., clenched teeth) and to recognize self-talk that reinforces anger.

Since the pregroup sessions had open membership, the addition of new group members each week necessitated the reiteration of the time out technique and basic information about the abuser treatment program. The older group members were encouraged to share their experiences during the week and discuss the effects the group had on their behavior or thoughts. The weekly pregroup preparation was also used to help the men set individual goals for themselves in the ongoing men's group.

Group leaders perceived several problems with the weekly pregroup format. Because the pregroup sessions lasted approximately an hour, the leaders often had insufficient time to engage group members beyond a brief check-in. The short group sessions also did not allow much interaction between the group members; group cohesion was not fostered. It appeared tedious for the older group members to hear the same material repeated for the newer group members. The pregroup was insufficiently structured for the presentation of educational/skill-developing information. The leaders of the pregroup sessions often differed from the leaders of the ongoing group. This made it more difficult for the pregroup members to join the ongoing groups co-facilitated by other group leaders.

Intensive Workshop Format

Due to the problems with the pregroup format, the group leaders felt a longer, more intensive session format was needed to engage the men in the group process. Thus the orientation workshop format was developed. The orientation workshop is conducted over two days, generally a Friday night and Saturday. The first session is approximately 3 1/2 hours long and the second session is approximately 8 1/2 hours long. In addition to the longer session, the orientation workshop is structured to include educational information and techniques described above as well as content that was previously excluded (e.g., a relaxation technique) because of time constraints. In addition, films illustrating the cycle of violence and the process of change are included. The addition of these activities provided the opportunity for greater interaction between the group members and the group leaders as well as among the group members themselves. The additional time spent on education familiarized the group members with the terminology and group process in order to help them assimilate more easily with the ongoing men's group.

RESULTS

Out of the 183 clients who completed intakes, 112 joined the pregroup or orientation workshop. The percentage of men who join each type of group preparation following intake is important as it is possible that the demands of attending an intensive workshop format would deter some men from participation in the program. Table 1 compares the percentage of men joining each type of preparation following intake. There was no significant difference between the weekly pregroup or intensive workshop formats.

Demographic information was examined using chi-square tests in order to determine the equivalence of the comparison groups on these variables. These demographic variables are considered important due to their possible effect on the drop-out rate. Marital status of the abuser may impact on the man's commitment to treatment. Separation, for example, may create an incentive to remain in treatment (e.g., to persuade the victim to return home). On the other hand, divorce may create a disincentive as a divorcing abuser often sees no reason to continue treatment. There is also the possibility that the completion rate of men who are not court-mandated treatment will differ from those who are ordered by the court to treatment. There were no significant differences found between the clients who joined the regular men's groups after the pregroup preparation and those who joined after the orientation workshops on the following factors: age, marital status, court status, and race (see Table 2).

A second important comparison is the rate of men who go on to join the ongoing groups following each type of preparation. Table 1 presents these comparisons. The rate of men who attended the weekly pregroup and then joined the ongoing group was 81.8%. The intensive workshop join rate was 89.7%. This difference was not statistically significant.

Finally, the hold rate (i.e., the percentage of men attending a set number of sessions prior to leaving the group) for each type of preparation was compared. Two hold rate criteria were used. The

Table 1

Comparisons of Join and Completion Rates

Joined Preparation Group Following Intake

	Yes	No	N	X2
Weekly	.63 (44)	.37 (26)	183	.1308
Intensive	.60 (68)	.40 (45)		

Joined On-Going Group Preparation

	Yes	No	N	X2
Weekly	.82 (36)	.18 (8)	112	1.4329
Intensive	.90 (61)	.10 (7)		

Completed 4 or More On-Going Sessions

	Yes	No	N	X2
Weekly	.57 (25)	.43 (19)	111	3.8437 *
Intensive	.75 (50)	.25 (17)		

Completed 10 or More On-Going Sessions

	Yes	No	N	X2
Weekly	.36 (16)	.64 (28)	112	2.0100
Intensive	.50 (34)	.50 (34)		

first criterion was the percentage of men completing four or more sessions. This criterion was chosen to provide comparable information to the Deschner and O'Neil study. Table 2 reveals that the four-session hold rate for the weekly pregroup preparation was 54.5%. The four-session hold rate for the intensive workshop was 74.6%. This was a statistically significant difference.

The second hold rate criterion was based on completion of 10 or

Table 2

Equivalence of Comparison Conditions at Intake

Marital Status of Participants

	Married	Unmarried	N	X2
Weekly	.84 (37)	.16 (7)	111	.4971
Intensive	.79 (53)	.21 (14)		

Court Status of Participants

	Court	Non-court	N	X2
Weekly	.36 (16)	.64 (28)	111	.1733
Intensive	.40 (27)	.60 (40)		

Race of Participants

	White	Non-white	N	X2
Weekly	.83 (30)	.17 (6)	94	.1447
Intensive	.86 (50)	.14 (8)		

more sessions. This criterion represented substantial participation in the program. Table 1 presents the comparison of the ten-session hold rates for each type of preparation. The ten-session hold rate for the weekly preparation was 36.3%. The intensive workshop has a 50.0% ten-session hold rate. While this difference was not statistically significant, it does show a continued clinically significant trend in favor of the orientation workshop.

DISCUSSION

While the design of the study limits strong inferences about the comparative effectiveness, group preparation does seem to play a role in engaging men who batter in the group process. The intensive workshop format appears to have a positive impact in reducing the drop-out rate, compared to a weekly preparation format. The intensive workshop format may decrease drop-outs in several ways. The more intensive and extended preparation time may be superior in providing information and skills needed to participate successfully in the ongoing group. Therefore, intensive workshop participants are likely to get off to a better start in making the transition to the ongoing group. Increased cohesion between members in the preparation cohort may facilitate continuation in the ongoing group. Each man enters the ongoing group with several other men he already knows, and to whom he feels some bond. In addition, the intensity of the weekend workshops gives a clear message about the need to make a commitment to the treatment process. Men going through such an experience may respond by making a firmer commitment to the program.

The study suggests the impact of the intensive workshop may diminish over time. This is not surprising, as the impact of preparation is most likely to be felt in the early stages of group participation. As time goes on, other group and individual factors would increase in saliency. The "good start" provided by pregroup preparation continues to have an important but diminished impact on continued participation.

The staff and the program may have improved over time, and this cannot be ruled out as a confounding factor in the study. Four of the seven men who did not join the ongoing men's groups after attending the orientation workshop had attended the first orientation workshop. All the men who attended workshops 4 through 8 went on to join the ongoing men's groups. Therefore, the superior completion rate may be due in part to improvement in staff rather than the format of the orientation per se.

In addition to decreased drop-outs, other feedback about the intensive workshops has been positive. The staff reported a noticeable increase in group interaction and participation. Further study is necessary, however, to determine the extent of the effectiveness of the orientation workshop approach.

One possible danger of the orientation workshop is that it may instill in the men a sense of having learned everything they need to know in order to control their abuse, and may result in premature drop-outs in some cases. This is an area that does warrant examination. Another issue is whether the orientation workshop better prepares those who eventually drop to remain violence free. Also, the issue of the fairly large drop-out rate prior to completion of the program still needs to be addressed, and additional strategies for reducing the drop-out rate developed.

As Brekke (in press) has pointed out, men who batter fit the profile of hard-to-reach clients. Modified versions of intensive workshops may also provide a preparatory group experience that will increase treatment participation, compliance, and efficacy for hard-to-reach clients. Weekend workshops are not the most convenient way to organize service, but intensive preparation could be cost-effective if it enhances treatment success, and engages clients more effectively than more traditional service formats.

As noted above, this quasi-experimental study leaves many threats to validity unanswered. On the other hand, the study demonstrates that research that can impact programmatic decision-making and further knowledge development in the field can be carried out with relatively little expenditure of resources, and little or no disruption to client service. While this study indicates that the intensive workshop format holds promise, further work is needed in order to understand the complex role of group preparation in the treatment of men who batter and other hard-to-reach clients.

REFERENCES

Anderson, Joseph D. (1987). Integrating research and practice in social work with groups. *Social Work with Groups, 9*, 111-122.

Bloom, Martin and Fischer, Joel (1982). *Evaluating practice: Guidelines for the accountable professional*. Englewood Cliffs, N.J.: Prentice-Hall.

Brekke, John (in press). The use of orientation groups for hard-to-reach clients: Model, method and evaluation. *Social Work with Groups*.

Deschner, Jeanne and O'Neil, John (1985). Lowering the dropout rate for groups for battering couples. Paper presented at the Symposium for the Advancement of Social Work with Groups, Chicago, Illinois.

Eddy, Melissa J. and Myers, Toby (1984). *Helping men who batter: A profile of programs in the U.S.* Texas Department of Human Resources.

Gondolf, Edward (1986). Evaluating programs for men who batter: Problems and perspectives. *Journal of Family Violence, 2*, 95-108.

Schecter, Susan (1983). *Women and male violence: The visions and struggles of the battered women's movement*. South End Press, Boston, MA.

Teaching Clients to Cope with Stress: The Effectiveness of Structured Group Stress Management Training

Richard M. Tolman
Sheldon D. Rose

SUMMARY. This study evaluated a structured group coping skills intervention designed to reduce stress. The treatment focused specifically on modifying cognitive mediation of events and on improving coping with ongoing routine stressors, and contained relaxation, cognitive restructuring, and social skill training components. The experimental treatment was compared to a relaxation-only treatment and to a waiting list control condition. Treated subjects significantly improved on three of four dependent measures of stress. Although no statistically significant differences were found between the conditions, the study provided support for further examination of the intervention.

The link between psychosocial stress and many emotional disorders and somatic illnesses has been well documented (see Dohrenwend and Dohrenwend, 1974, Kiritz and Moos, 1974; Lipowski, 1977). Social workers aware of the link between stress and various problems may attempt to prevent or treat stress-related disorders by improving an individual's ability to deal with those stressors. Re-

Richard M. Tolman, PhD, is Assistant Professor, Jane Addams College of Social Work, University of Illinois at Chicago, Chicago, IL 60680, and Sheldon D. Rose, PhD, is Professor, School of Social Work, University of Wisconsin, Madison, WI 53706.

The research on which this article is based was supported in part by a grant from the University of Wisconsin-Madison Alumni Research Foundation. Preparation of this article was supported in part by a National Institute of Mental Health Grant 1T32-MH17152-01 awarded to Richard M. Tolman. Address correspondence to Richard M. Tolman.

cent years have seen a rapid increase in interest in stress management techniques. Purveyors of stress reduction programs bombard the public with approaches as diverse as exercise classes, special diets, yoga and meditation, drugs and vitamins, hypnosis, and progressive relaxation. Research evaluating the effectiveness of these various approaches can help practitioners make critical judgments about the usefulness of various stress management techniques for their clients.

This study evaluated the efficacy of a structured group cognitive-behavioral approach to stress management. The development of the approach and its theoretical underpinnings have been described in detail elsewhere (Tolman and Rose, 1985) and will be briefly described here. The multiple-method stress management treatment program (MM) was developed at the Interpersonal Skills Training and Research Project at the University of Wisconsin, School of Social Work. In order to develop a treatment approach that social workers could apply to the broad range of concerns presented by their clients, existing stress management approaches were reviewed. This review and a series of clinical pilot studies resulted in a treatment program which integrates several different stress management techniques, relaxation, cognitive restructuring and social skills training, into a structured time-limited group format. These components and the unique features of MM are discussed below.

Relaxation approaches to stress management aim at reducing physiological arousal to stressors. The relaxation approach included in MM emphasizes the teaching of abbreviated progressive relaxation techniques (Bernstein and Given, 1984) to reduce chronic stress reactions by relaxing at specific intervals, and the use of relaxation techniques which can aid coping with acute arousal, such as a diaghramatic breathing technique. (Everly and Rosenfeld, 1981).

Stress theorists (Lazarus and Launier, 1978; Cameron and Meichenbaum, 1982) have emphasized the transactional nature of stress. This view posits that one's cognitive appraisal of a stressor mediates one's response to that stressor. From this framework, a client's perceptions of both the stressfulness of a situation and of her or his ability to successfully cope with a situation become targets of intervention. Based on the work of Meichenbaum (1977), Ellis (1970), and Beck (1976), the cognitive restructuring component of the stress management treatment focuses on direct modification of cognitions that are viewed as dysfunctional or non-adaptive.

Individuals' attempts to cope with stressors can be focused on attempts to modify the environment itself. Clients can be taught skills which can improve their ability to change their environments. As many of the stressors that clients report are interpersonal in nature, social skills, particularly assertion training, are particularly relevant to stress management. A widely shared clinical observation is that the inability to express emotions effectively is linked to psychosomatic illness. Assertiveness training may be effective in the reduction of such illness (see discussion in Stoyva and Anderson, 1982). Social skills training has considerable support as to its efficacy in changing interpersonal behavior and in reducing anxiety (see reviews by Alberti, 1977; Twentyman and Zimmering, 1978; Bellack and Hersen, 1979).

The MM approach has several distinctive features. The focus of treatment is on coping with routine stressors rather than major life events. There is evidence that frequent daily stressful situations that to some degree characterize everyday transactions with the environment are more closely linked to and may have a greater effect on moods and health than major undesirable life events (Kanner, Coyne, Schaefer and Lazarus, 1981). Clients are trained to recognize their routine stressors and to modify their response to the stressors.

Although the MM approach is highly structured, the program combines training in the component skills with individualized application. Group members bring descriptions of problem situations they are encountering to the group. Through discussion, problem-solving, role-playing, and homework assignments clients learn to apply the skills to their particular circumstances.

Cognitive-behavioral treatment approaches have generally ignored group process as relevant to treatment outcome (Rose, Tolman and Tallant, 1985). The MM approach emphasizes the group as a means rather than as a context of change. Careful attention is given to maximizing participation, involvement and appropriate self-disclosure of members, to building cohesion among group members, and to encouraging positive group norms.

A short-term structured group treatment for stress has a number of advantages as a social work intervention. Clients need not commit themselves to a lengthy, costly process. The structured nature of intervention makes training of leaders a simpler, more replicable process. Effective dissemination of such an approach is more feasible than that of complex, poorly defined treatments. The set of skills taught in MM are broadly applicable, flexible, and presumably generalizable to a great many problems facing the clients to whom social workers address their helping efforts. Because treatment is provided in groups, service is cost-effective.

In this study, the integrated multi-method stress management treatment was compared to a credible alternative treatment. The alternative treatment was a similarly structured program which utilized only relaxation training techniques. It was hypothesized that the combination of relaxation, cognitive, and behavioral techniques would be more effective in helping clients to cope with routine stressors than would relaxation alone. Related studies support this hypothesis (see review by Lehrer and Woolfolk, 1984). Both treatments were compared to a control group of subjects who requested treatment but were placed on a waiting list. It was hypothesized that subjects in both treatments would show greater improvement on stress measures than the waiting list subjects.

METHOD

Subjects

Subjects were recruited from the general public via posters, newspaper advertisements, and through social service agencies likely to have contact with people experiencing difficulties dealing with stress. In all, 45 subjects who identified themselves as needing stress management training completed pregroup interviews. Subjects were initially interviewed by one of nine graduate student interviewers. The interviewers screened subjects who were inappropriate for treatment, explained experimental procedures, gathered demographic, and other relevant clinical data to be used by the leaders, and administered the pretest measures.

One subject was deemed inappropriate for the study because she presented herself as desiring an opportunity to learn stress management techniques to aid her in her social work practice. Three subjects dropped out of the study prior to the start of treatment. The total number of subjects participating in the study was reduced to 41.

The mean age of the subjects was 36.3. The mean education in years was 15.6, indicating a relatively well-educated group. Twenty-nine subjects were women, and 12 were men. All subjects were Caucasian, with the exception of one Asian man. A third of the subjects (14) were professionals. The other subjects were somewhat evenly represented in technical (4), clerical (7), student (6), unemployed (5) and other categories (5).

The types of stress that subjects were experiencing were quite varied. In response to a pretest interview question about the stressors that led them to seek help, the largest category was difficulties in interpersonal relationships. In all 23 subjects listed 44 different interpersonal stressors, including having little social life or feeling lonely (8), separation, divorce or remarriage issues (7), addiction or other health problems of family members (6), and death of family members (4). The next largest category was work and school-related problems. Twenty-three subjects named 27 total stressors, for example added responsibilities, impending layoffs, unemployment, and domineering employers. Seventeen subjects reported 25 intrapersonal stressors, for example setting unrealistic goals, lack of direction, and inability to express feelings. The fourth largest category was health related problems. In all eight subjects listed 12 different health problems including hypertension, ulcers, back problems, fatigue, gout, PMS, and diet problems. Finally, 11 subjects reported financial difficulties as major stressors leading them to seek intervention. It can be seen from this brief description that the subjects were heterogenous in their stress-related problems. Stressors named as major concerns included both major life crises, as well as more chronic, daily hassles.

Design

The study used an experimental between-groups design, comparing the MM treatment to a relaxation-only (RO) control, and a waiting list (WL) control group. Following the completion of all the pregroup interviews, subjects deemed appropriate for treatment were randomly assigned to the treatment conditions, blocking for sex and preference for meeting time.

Two MM and two RO groups were conducted. Two leaders, the first author and an experienced graduate student, each led one MM and one RO group to control for a leader confound. The treatment groups met once per week for eight weeks. One week following the eighth session, the posttest evaluation was administered to all subjects. Three months after posttest, a follow-up evaluation was administered to the MM and RO subjects. Comparison of follow-up results for the WL subjects are not relevant as those subjects began treatment following the initial eight-week waiting period.

Multi-Method Treatment

The MM groups met for eight weekly two-hour sessions. Early sessions focused on skill acquisition. Later sessions emphasized discussion of hassles experienced by members. Group time was spent in helping members choose and implement effective strategies to cope with the difficulties they were experiencing. The three basic skill components were introduced sequentially. Relaxation skills were introduced in sessions 1 and 2. Cognitive restructuring was introduced in sessions 3, 4 and 5. Social skills were introduced in sessions 6 and 7.

The relaxation component of the program incorporated the following:

1. Introduction of the concept of relaxation as a skill that can be used to decrease arousal due to stress and as an activity that can minimize the deleterious effects of stress.
2. Through demonstration and guided practice, teaching the skill of progressive relaxation, which is used as a regular activity to decrease overall arousal.
3. Institution of relaxation as a homework assignment on a regular basis.
4. Introduction of relaxation as a skill for coping with a specific stressor and the use of relaxation:
   a. before an anticipated stressor, to reduce tension felt while waiting and to maximize effective performance in the situation.

    b. during a stressful event, to decrease arousal that is interfering with performance.

    c. after a stressful event, to reduce the tension or arousal resulting from the specific event.

5. Through demonstration and guided practice, teaching relaxation as a coping skill in specific situations by differential relaxation (the tensing and relaxation of specified muscle groups), by short-cut relaxation (the pairing of deep breathing with tensing of muscles), and by pairing stress-reducing self-statements with the breathing techniques.

6. Role-play of stressful situations and practice through role-play, in relaxation techniques for coping.

7. Application of relaxation to actual stressful events in the environment through homework assignments.

The cognitive approach applied in the study involved the following procedures:

1. Explanation of the relationship between self-defeating self-statements and self-enhancing, or coping self-statements.

2. Through exercises, training the client to differentiate between self-defeating self-statements and self-enhancing or coping self-statements.

3. Identification of the client's self-defeating statements and irrational self-evaluations.

4. Generation of alternative adaptive, or coping statements to replace self-defeating statements and irrational self-evaluations.

5. Replacement of self-defeating thoughts with coping thoughts through cognitive modeling and rehearsal.

6. Practice of new ways of thinking through goal-directed homework assignments.

The social skill training component of the MM program consisted of the following procedures:

1. Explanation of the relationship between social skills deficits and stress.

2. Identification of social deficits through training exercises in commonly occurring social events.

3. Identification of specific stress-filled events unique to each client.
4. Determination of goals, critical moment, and specific behavior required to deal with the event effectively.
5. Behavioral modeling of the event.
6. Behavioral rehearsal by the client, with and without coaching of the new response.
7. Structured feedback to the client.
8. Discussion of the specific situation by linking it to general stress problems.
9. Application of newly learned social skills in the environment through successively more difficult homework assignments.

All sessions followed a similar format. Goals and agenda for the sessions were reviewed. Evaluations of the previous session were reviewed and questions or group problems were discussed. Leaders reviewed homework assignments and addressed problems with completion. In later sessions, the leaders encouraged members to share successful application of skills. Sharing assignment completion and successful use of techniques provided an opportunity for the leaders and group members to give social reinforcement. Members were also encouraged to give positive feedback and suggestions to other members. Leaders then introduced skills, through a brief lecture and a structured exercise. Members practiced skills in the group, and received a homework assignment relating to the skill. A ten-minute break was taken at the middle of each session, to allow time for the member to informally socialize. At the end of each session, members filled out a postsession questionnaire discussed below.

Relaxation-Only Treatment

The relaxation-only (RO) treatment was based on the progressive relaxation technique described by Borkovec and Bernstein (1973), and followed the relaxation procedures described above with several variations. Additional relaxation skills were also taught, including meditation techniques (the client focuses on breathing by using a mental device, e.g., the word "one" as he or she breathes out) and imaginal techniques (the client constructs a mental image of a scene associated with relaxation, utilizing sensory modalities such as picturing the scene and recreating the smells and touches and sounds associated with the scene. The use of relaxation paired with self-statements was excluded. Because fewer skills were taught, more time was spent in repeated group practice of the relaxation skills.

As in the MM, the RO condition combined structured exercises with individualized instruction in how to appropriately use techniques. Hillenberg and Collins (1982), in an extensive review of the relaxation literature, identified three procedural considerations which appear to increase the efficacy of training: a minimum of four sessions, live rather than taped instructions, and utilization of home practice. The RO condition contained all three of these procedural considerations.

The RO groups also met for eight two-hour weekly sessions. The sessions followed the same format described in the MM condition. The use of similar agendas and exercise formats in both the MM and RO groups balanced both conditions for structure and member participation.

Dependent Measures

Profile of Mood States

Negative affect has come to be accepted among stress researchers as prima facie evidence of the presence of stress (Derogatis, 1982). In order to tap the range of emotional states that may have been relevant for subjects in this study, a multidimensional scale was used. The Profile of Mood States (POMS) (McNair, Lorr and Droppleman, 1971) is a 65-item, 5-point adjective rating scale designed to measure six transient fluctuating affect states: Tension-Anxiety, Depression-Dejection, Anger-Hostility, Vigor-Activity, Fatigue-Inertia, and Confusion-Bewilderment. In addition, a total mood disturbance score derived from the six subscales can be presumed to be highly reliable because of intercorrelations among the six primary factors. The POMS has been shown to have good internal consistency reliability and adequate test-retest reliability (McNair and Lorr, 1964), and similar factor structure and loadings in a number of studies (Lorr, McNair and Weinstein, 1963, McNair and Lorr, 1964). In addition, the POMS has been sensitive to change in various therapeutic approaches and discriminated between no-treatment, psychotherapy and hospitalized groups (Imber, 1975). The POMS was administered at pretest, posttest and follow-up.

SCL-90-R

In addition to negative affect, a wide range of symptoms have been attributed to the presence of stress. The idiosyncratic nature of individual stress reactions requires that a multidimensional measure be used to tap the range of symptoms that may occur in a diverse sample. The SCL-90-R is a self-report symptom inventory designed to measure symptomatic psychological distress. The inventory yields scores on nine primary symptom dimensions and three global indices of distress. Somatization, Obsessive-Compulsive, Interpersonal Sensitivity, Depression, Anxiety, Hostility, Phobic Anxiety, Paranoid Ideation, and Psychoticism are the primary symptom constructs. The General Severity Index, which combines information on the number of symptoms and intensity of distress was used in statistical analysis in this study. Two other global indices can be derived: The positive symptom total, which reflects only the total symptoms, and the positive symptoms distress index, which is a pure intensity measure, adjusted for the number of symptoms.

The SCL-90-R has been sensitive to change in a variety of clinical and medical contexts including depression (Weissman, Slobetz, Prusoff, Mezritz and Howard, 1976; Weissman, Pottenger, Kleber, Rubin, Williams and Thompson, 1977) sexual disorders, (Derogatis, Meyer and King, 1981) psychopharmacological treatment of chronic anxiety disorders, (Kathol, Noyes, Slymen, Crowe, Clancy and Kerber, 1980) and in stress research (Carrington, Collings, Benson, Robinson, Wood, Lehrer, Woolfolk and Cole, 1980; Horowitz, Wilner, Kaltreider and Alvarez, 1980). The SCL-90-R has demonstrated high levels of test-retest and internal consistency reliability (Derogatis, 1978; Edwards, Yarvis, Mueller, Zingale and Wagman, 1978). The SCL-90-R was administered at pretest, posttest, and follow-up.

Daily Hassles Scale

The Hassles Scale (Kanner, Coyne, Schaefer and Lazarus, 1981) is a 117 item scale which samples hassles from work, family, friends, the environment, practical considerations, and chance oc-currences. The instructions ask subjects to identify hassles they have experienced over the past month and to rate the severity of each hassle on a three-point scale. The test-retest correlations with a normal population not selected for stress were .79 for frequency of hassles (Kanner et al., 1981). The hassles severity index, the sum of all item ratings, was used in evaluation of the stress management program because it includes both the frequency of hassles and their relative severity.

Self-Monitoring

All subjects were asked to monitor their average distress level on a ten-point scale (1 = no distress; 10 = highest distress) three times daily during a one-week period following the pretest period, and for one-week at the end of treatment. Because of poor comple-tion rates by untreated subjects, comparisons are available only be-tween subjects in the two treatment conditions and it was decided not to ask subjects to self-monitor prior to the follow-up evaluation.

Measures of the Independent Variable

The unique interactions that take place in the group setting can account for some of the variance in treatment outcome. Certain group processes such as self-disclosure or cohesion may be neces-sary and/or sufficient conditions for therapeutic change. Widely dif-fering process between treatment groups confounds the interpreta-tion of results in treatment comparison studies. Group processes specific to the individual groups, rather than treatment techniques themselves, may account for differential change between treat-ments.

Expectancy for improvement and credibility of treatment are also factors which if not balanced equally between treatment conditions confound inferences about treatment effects. If treatment differ-ences between the MM and RO conditions are found, measures of group process, clients' expectations for change, and the credibility of the treatment provide data to assess the contribution of group process to the outcome.

A 14-item self-report measure developed by the authors for this study was completed after each session. The questionnaire explored self-disclosure, involvement and participation in the group, cohesion, satisfaction, usefulness of the session, and the members' expectation for improvement as a result of the treatment. Subjects responded to items on Likert scales. A typical item was "The concerns I discussed today were (1 = not at all personal; 6 = extremely personal)." The usefulness and satisfaction ratings provided a measure of credibility.

Planned Analysis

Wilcoxon signed-rank tests on matched pairs were used to evaluate within-condition changes for the MM, RO, and WL conditions. To evaluate differences between conditions at posttest and follow-up, non-parametric ANCOVA contrasts were done, using pretest scores as covariates, and sex and treatment condition as factors. Sex was used as a factor because drop-outs from the study following random assignment left men and women unequally distributed in the treatment conditions despite the efforts to block for sex.

The ANCOVA procedure allows for a more powerful test of treatment differences because variance due to sex and pretest scores are removed prior to testing the differences due to treatment. Non-parametric ANCOVA is the preferred procedure because in cases of normal distributions, non-parametric ANCOVA is almost as powerful as its parametric analogue. However, in non-normal distributions, non-parametric ANCOVA has greater power (Olejnik and Algina, 1984).

Pair-wise contrasts of treatment conditions were accomplished using regression with dummy codes. This procedure entails deriving codes such that the B coefficients represent the actual difference in treatment mean rank scores. The dependent measure is then regressed simultaneously on the covariates and set of dummy codes. Testing the B coefficient is equivalent to testing the significance of the treatment contrast. Experimental type 1 error was controlled by using the Dunn-Bonferoni method. The tests of planned contrasts were one-tailed.

RESULTS

Table 1 presents the mean test scores for all three conditions at pretest, posttest, and follow-up. The Wilcoxon signed-rank tests revealed that all three conditions improved from pretest to posttest on the GSI index. However, only the MM and RO improved significantly on the POMS and Hassles measure.

The MM and RO conditions maintained significant improvement from pretest to follow-up on the symptom, mood and hassles measures. Neither the MM or RO improved significantly on the self-monitoring measure, although the MM condition changed in a positive direction, while the RO condition showed change in a negative direction.

The non-parametric ANCOVA pair-wise contrasts revealed that neither treatment was superior to waiting list controls at posttest, nor did the MM and RO treatments significantly differ at posttest or follow-up on any of the dependent measures.

Posthoc Analysis

The failure to find significant differences between the treatment groups and waiting list led to post hoc exploration of the data. It was hypothesized that the improvement of the waiting list might be due to waiting list subjects seeking alternative treatment during the waiting period. Interviews after the eight-week waiting period confirmed that five of the thirteen waiting list subjects did participate in some form of counseling or other organized self-improvement activity during the waiting period. The data were then examined, separating the treated and untreated waiting list subjects into two groups. Table 2 presents these results. Mann-Whitney tests of the relevant pair-wise contrasts revealed no significant differences between the MM and RO conditions and the untreated controls on any of the measures.

Data from the postsession questionnaire were collected in order to rule out the hypotheses that group process, expectancy and credi-

TABLE 1. Mean Scores on Dependent Measures

	PRE	POST	FOLLOW-UP
SCL-90-R			
MM (n=13)			
X	.924	.515*	.387*
SD	.559	.565	.267
RO (n=14)			
X	1.055	.566	.767*
SD	.665	.533	.942
WL (n=14)			
X	1.030	.692*	
SD	.545	.443	
POMS			
MM			
X	54.5	44.6*	44.9*
SD	6.3	10.5	10.4
RO			
X	55.4	46.9*	47.3*
SD	7.9	8.1	10.1
WL			
X	55.7	51.9	
SD	11.1	10.1	
HASSLES			
MM			
X	56.2	31.0*	19.4*
SD	29.0	23.9	11.0
RO			
X	62.4	36.5*	24.5*
SD	46.1	29.5	17.0
WL			
X	54.9	42.9	
SD	34.7	29.8	
SELF-MONITOR			
MM			
X	3.6	3.4	
SD	1.3	1.6	
RO			
X	3.7	4.2	
SD	1.5	0.8	

*Indicates Wilcoxon signed rank for pretest to posttest or follow-up is significant ($p < .05$) (Dunn-Bonferoni test). No pair-wise contrasts were significant.

TABLE 2. Mean Pre to Post Difference Scores for MM, RO, Treated WL and Untreated WL Subjects

	SCL	POMS	HASSLES
MM	.41	9.9	25.2
RO	.43	8.6	25.9
Treated WL	.30	4.3	12.2
Untreated WL	.40	3.2	11.6

bility of treatment accounted for treatment differences. Because no treatment differences between the MM and RO conditions were found, this data was not extensively examined at this time. An examination of the mean scores by group by session for each questionnaire item indicated only very trivial differences in group process ratings, and similar expectancies and credibility ratings for the treatments. However, the subjects consistently rated both groups highly in terms of positive group attributes. Additional information about group process comes from structured post-group interviews. Clients in both conditions credited support from the group as promoting change in their coping skills and in reducing stress directly.

Clinical Significance

The self-report of subjects in groups and in posttest interviews indicated that many subjects made notable changes which they attributed to the treatment. However additional criteria were sought to determine if the changes were clinically significant. The SCL and POMS scores of subjects were compared to those of outpatient psychiatric patients. Such norms are available for the SCL and POMS measures, which provide separate norms for male and female patients.

Table 3 presents the mean scores on the GSI measure for each condition in the form of T-scores derived from those norms. The T-score format is a useful one in that it allows comparisons to be made between subscales and between measures in comparable units. In addition, T-scores have a mean of 50, and standard deviation of 10,

TABLE 3. SCL-90-R General Symptom Index Outpatient T-Scores

	PRE	POST	FOLLOW-UP
MM	45	38	36
RO	47	41	44
WL	47	42	

making it relatively easy to compare scores as to their distance from the outpatient mean. For ease of presentation a combined T score was created by taking a weighted average of the male and female T-scores. GSI T-scores for the entire population indicate that subjects began the study at levels which were characteristic of a clinical population, although slightly below the mean of the outpatient norm population. At posttest the MM condition reduced to levels over a full standard deviation below the norm population. The relaxation condition made similar gains. The waiting list controls, while making more modest gains, also reduced over one-half standard deviation.

Norms are not available for the POMS mood disturbance index but they are available for each of the subscales (Table 4). Initial levels for the subscales show that each of the conditions had mood levels that were at the mean of the outpatient population. One exception was the vigor score, which was initially one-half standard deviation above the outpatient norms mean score. The subscales data reflect pre-post gains for the treatment group from one-half to one standard deviation on all subscales. The waiting list control group showed more modest gains, ranging from about one-half standard deviation on the anger subscale to a slight deterioration on the fatigue scale.

DISCUSSION

The results of the statistical analysis indicate that treated subjects showed significant improvement on three of four dependent measures. These improvements were demonstrably clinically significant. However, the subjects receiving the MM treatment showed no

TABLE 4. Profile of Mood States Subscale Outpatient T-Scores

	PRE	POST	FOLLOW–UP
TENSION			
MM	50	41	38
RO	49	41	40
WL	50	45	
DEPRESSION			
MM	47	40	38
RO	47	42	42
WL	47	43	
ANGER			
MM	49	43	43
RO	52	48	48
WL	56	52	
FATIGUE			
MM	50	45	46
RO	54	45	45
WL	54	50	
CONFUSION			
MM	48	39	38
RO	50	42	41
WL	50	43	
VIGOR			
MM	58	62	56
RO	56	61	56
WL	57	57	

greater improvement than did subjects in the RO treatment. Although change scores were in the predicted direction on every measure, comparisons of the MM and RO treatments with the WL condition were not statistically significant. These results did not support the prediction that both treatments would be superior to the waiting list in reducing stress.

These results raise the question of why the waiting list condition subjects improved as much as they did. Post hoc statistical analysis did not indicate that the control subjects' improvement could be attributed to alternative treatment seeking. One possibility is that the knowledge that help was on the way may have reduced stress during the waiting period. Another possible explanation is a "John Henry effect." The effect refers to the possibility that subjects not receiving treatment may respond with attempts to prove they can do as well on their own. Some anecdotal evidence from interviews with waiting list subjects supports this hypothesis.

An alternative explanation is that the pretest interview itself may have been an effective intervention. At pretest subjects were asked to talk at length about stressors in their lives, and about stress-related symptoms they were experiencing. The pretesting may have sensitized control subjects to areas which needed attention, and possibly provided clues as to effective strategies for addressing those areas.

Finally, it cannot be ruled out that the improvement of the waiting list, and possibly the treated subjects was due largely to naturally occurring processes. Stress symptoms may be cyclical and remiss without external intervention over a period of weeks. Longer term follow-up may have revealed that treatment was superior in the maintenance of stress reduction.

It was expected that the MM treatment would bring about longer lasting changes than the RO treatment for several reasons. First, by providing subjects with a greater variety of skills to apply in stressful situations, subjects would be more likely to have a technique available to meet unexpected contingencies. Second, unlike relaxation skills, the cognitive techniques are more readily used and maintained without the need for a specific practice time. Third, the use of interpersonal change techniques are likely to bring about lasting environmental changes which would decrease stress for the subject.

MM subjects did continue to improve from posttest to follow-up on the symptom measure, while the RO subjects deteriorated. MM subjects maintained their gains on the mood measure, while the RO subjects deteriorated. This evidence of a maintenance effect for the MM approach however was not statistically significant.

The participants identified the group experience itself as an important component of the change process. While differences between the conditions were trivial and not explored statistically, the study indicates that group process is an important component of treatment success. Further research should be directed at further exploring the contribution of group process to successful outcome.

Multidimensional measures were chosen for this investigation in order to cover the broad range of relevant problems that subjects present when seeking treatment. This strategy may have masked significant improvements in the areas that were most important to each subject. Individualized measures for each subject could be added in future investigations. On the other hand, treatment could be administered to a narrower population. Populations in previous studies have been more homogenous in terms of presenting symptom e.g., test anxiety or in terms of a demographic characteristic e.g., dental students. Narrowing the population served can increase the precision with which treatment is administered. Techniques may be geared to the specific population studied. Group members may be more likely to be of specific help to each other because of similarity of their experiences.

Although differences between the MM, RO, and WL conditions were not statistically significant, the mean differences were in the predicted directions. This suggests that if the study had more power, the null hypothesis of no differences between treated subjects and waiting list controls could have been rejected. This argument, of course, can be made about any study where differences in the predicted direction are present, however small or insignificant. The appeal in this case to insufficient power is more valid for two reasons. The differences between treated subjects and waiting list controls were not clinically trivial. Second, pre-experimental power calculations based on pilot data indicated that the sample size chosen for this experiment was sufficient to reject the null hypothesis had the waiting list control group not shown improvement. Future studies should use a sample size sufficient to achieve enough power to reject the null hypothesis based on the effect size demonstrated in this study. It should be clarified perhaps that this argument about power is not made to increase the reader's confidence that the MM treatment is effective, but rather that future investigation of the approach is warranted by these results.

The finding that subjects receiving stress management treatment made statistically and clinically significant improvements was consistent with previous pilot work. Further study will determine whether or not the smaller but notable improvement of waiting list subjects is a consistent pattern. The results of this study, in the context of the body of work supporting the intervention evaluated in this study, are promising enough to warrant further efforts to examine the multi-method approach.

REFERENCES

Alberti, R.E. (1977). *Assertiveness: Innovations, applications, issues*. San Luis Obispo, California: Impact Publishers.

Beck, A.T. (1976). *Cognitive therapy and the emotional disorders*. New York: International Universities Press.

Bellack A.S. and Hersen, M.M. (Eds.) (1979). *Research and Practice in Social Skills Training*. New York: Plenum Press.

Bernstein D.A. and Borkovec, T.D. (1973). *Progressive Relaxation Training: A Manual for the Helping Professions*. Chicago: Research Press.

Bernstein D.A. and Given, B.A. (1984). Progressive relaxation: Abbreviated methods. In R.L. Woolfolk and P.M. Lehrer (Eds.), *Principles and practice of stress management*, (pp. 43-69) New York: The Guilford Press.

Cameron R. and Meichenbaum, D. (1982). The nature of effective coping and the treatment of stress related problems: A cognitive-behavioral perspective. In L. Goldberger and S. Breznitz (Eds.), *Handbook of Stress*, New York: Free Press.

Carrington, P., Collings, G.H., Benson, H., Robinson, H., Wood, L.W., Lehrer, P.M., Woolfolk, R.L. and Cole, J.W. (1980). The use of meditation-relaxation techniques for the management of stress in a working population. *Journal of Occupational Medicine, 22*, 221-231.

Charlesworth, E.A., Murphy, S. and Beutler, L.E. (1982). Stress management skill for nursing students. *Journal of Clinical Psychology, 23*, 761-768.

Decker, T.W., Williams, J.M. and Hall, D. (1982). Preventive training in management of stress for reduction of physiological symptoms through increased cognitive and behavioral controls. *Psychological Reports, 50*, 1327-1334.

Derogatis, L.R. (1975). *SCL-90-R administration, scoring and procedures manual, Vol. 1.* Baltimore: Clinical Psychometric Research.

Derogatis, L.R. (1982). Self-report measures of stress. In L. Goldberger and S. Breznitz, *Handbook of stress: Theoretical and clinical aspects.* New York: Free Press.

Derogatis, L.R., Meyer, J.K. and King, K.M. (1981). Psychopathology in individuals with sexual dysfunction. *American Journal of Psychiatry, 138,* 757-763.

Dohrenwend B.S. and Dohrenwend, B.P. (1974). *Stressful life events: Their nature and effects.* New York: John Wiley and Sons.

Edwards, D.W., Yarvis, R.M., Mueller, B.P., Zingale, H.C. and Wagman, W.J. (1978). Test-taking and the stability of adjustment scales. *Evaluation Quarterly, 2,* 275-291.

Everly G.S. and Rosenfeld, R. (1981). *The nature and treatment of the stress response: A practical guide for clinicians.* New York: Plenum Press.

Forman, S.G. (1981). Stress management training: Evaluation of effects on school psychological services. *Journal of School Psychology, 19,* 233-241.

Forman, S.G. (1982). Stress management for teachers: A cognitive-behavioral program. *Journal of School Psychology, 20,* 180-187.

Haskell, D., Pugatch, D. and McNair, D.M. (1969). Time-limited psychotherapy for whom? *Archives of General Psychiatry, 21,* 546-552.

Hillenberg J.B. and Collins, F. (1982). A procedural analysis and review of relaxation training research. *Behavioural Research and Therapy, 20,* 251-260.

Holroyd, K.A., Appel, M.A. and Andrasik, F. (1983). A cognitive-behavioral approach to psychophysiological disorders. In D. Meichenbaum and M.E. Jaremko (Eds.), *Stress reduction and prevention.* New York: Plenum Press.

Horowitz, M.J., Wilner, N., Kaltreider, N. and Alvarez, W. (1980). Signs and symptoms of posttraumatic stress disorder. *Archives of General Psychiatry, 37,* 85-92.

Imber, S.D. (1975). Patient direct self-report techniques. In I.E. Waskow and M.B. Parloff, (Eds.), *Psychotherapy change measures.* Rockville, Maryland: National Institute of Mental Health.

Kanner, A.D., Coyne, J., Schaefer, C. and Lazarus, R.S. (1981). Comparison of two modes of stress measurement: Daily hassles and uplifts versus major life events. *Journal of Behavioral Medicine, 4,* 1-39.

Kathol, R.G., Noyes, R., Slymen, D.J., Crowe, R.R., Clancy, J. and Kerber, R.E. (1980). Propand in chronic anxiety disorders. *Archives of General Psychiatry, 37,* 1361-1365.

Kiritz S. and Moos, R.H. (1974). Physiological effects of the social environment. *Psychosomatic Medicine, 36,* 96-114.

Lazarus R.S. and Launier, R. (1978). Stress-related transactions between person and environment. In L.A. Peruin and M. Lewis (Eds.), *Perspectives in interactional psychology* (pp. 287-327). New York: Plenum Press.

Lehrer P.M. and Woolfolk, R.L. (1984). Are stress reduction techniques interchangeable, or do they have specific effects?: A review of the comparative empirical literature. In R.L. Woolfolk and P.M. Lehrer (Eds.), *Principles and practice of stress management*. New York: The Guilford Press.

Lorr, M., McNair, D.M. and Weinstein, G.J. (1963). Early effects of chlordiazepoxide (Librium) used with psychotherapy. *Journal of Psychiatric Research, 1*, 257-270.

Lustman, P.J. and Sowa, C.J. (1983). Comparative efficacy of biofeedback and stress inoculation for stress reduction. *Journal of Clinical Psychology, 39*, 191-197.

McNair, D.M. and Lorr, M. (1964). An analysis of mood in neurotics. *Journal of Abnormal and Social Psychology, 69*, 620-627.

McNair, D.M., Lorr, M. and Droppleman, L.F. (1971). *Profile of mood states*. San Diego: Educational and Industrial Testing Service.

Meichenbaum, D. (1977). *Cognitive-behavior modification: An integrative approach*. New York: Plenum Press.

Meichenbaum, D. and Cameron, R. (1972). Stress inoculation: A skills training approach to anxiety management. Unpublished manuscript, University of Waterloo, 1972.

Novaco, R.W. (1976). Treatment of chronic anger through cognitive and relaxation controls. *Journal of Consulting and Clinical Psychology, 44*, 681.

Olejnik S.F. and Algina, J. (1984). Parametric ANCOVA vs. rank transform ANCOVA when assumptions of conditional normality and homoscedasticity are violated. Paper presented at the American Association for Educational Research, New Orleans.

Rose, S.D., Tolman, R.M. and Tallant, S. (1985). Group process in cognitive-behavioral therapy. *The Behavior Therapist, 8*, 71-75.

Stoyva J. and Anderson, C. (1982) A coping-rest model of relaxation and stress management. In L. Goldberger and S. Breznitz (Eds.), *Handbook of Stress*. New York: Free Press.

Tisdelle, D.A., Hansen, D.J., St. Lawrence, J.S., Kelly, J.A. and Brown, J.C. (1983, December). Stress management for dental students: A multimodal approach. Paper presented at the Association for the Advancement of Behavior Therapy, Washington, D.C.

Tolman R.M. and Rose, S.D. (1985). Coping with stress: A multimodal approach. *Social Work, 30*, 151-158.

Turk, D.C. (1978). Application of coping skills training to the treatment of pain. In C.D. Spielberger and I.G. Sarason (Eds.), *Stress and anxiety, Vol. 5*. New York: Brunner/Mazel.

Twentyman, C.T. and Zimmering, R.T. (1978). Behavioral training of social skills: A critical review. In M. Hersen, R. Eisler, and P. Miller (Eds.), *Progress in behavior modification, Vol. 7*. New York: Academic Press.

Weissman, N.M., Pottenger, M., Kleber, H., Ruben, H.L., Williams, D. and Thompson, W.D. (1977). Symptom patterns in primary and secondary depression: A comparison of primary depressives with depressed opiate addicts, alcoholics, and schizophrenics. *Archives of General Psychiatry, 34*, 854-862.

Life Skills Training with Mothers of Handicapped Children

Maura A. Kirkham
Robert F. Schilling II

SUMMARY. This paper describes a life skills training intervention with 230 mothers of children with a variety of developmental disabilities. The study's design evaluated the effects of a skills-building method developed to improve coping and social support networks of mothers of handicapped children. In groups of 10-12, mothers of handicapped children participated in one of two intervention groups: a skills-building intervention or a comparison treatment intervention using traditional counseling methods. At posttest assessment participants in the skills-building sessions demonstrated improved coping and communication skills, greater satisfaction with social support networks, and a reduction in depression and stress levels.

Over time, a variety of stressful events impact the life of many families. Illness, divorce, death, chronic unemployment, interpersonal discord, and developmental disability tax the family's personal and environmental resources. Helping families develop resources and skills to cope with these problems has always been consonant with the mission of social work (Hartman, 1981). This

Maura A. Kirkham, PhD, is Assistant Professor, School of Social Work, 425 Henry Mall, University of Wisconsin-Madison, Madison, WI 53706. Robert F. Schilling, PhD, is Assistant Professor, School of Social Work, Columbia University, 622 West 113th Street, New York, NY 10025. Requests for reprints should be sent to Dr. Kirkham.

This research project was funded by grant number MCJ 530513 from the Maternal and Child Health Research Branch, Bureau of Health Care Delivery and Assistance, U.S. Public Health Service, Department of Health and Human Services and grant 90 CA 1159 from the National Center on Child Abuse and Neglect.

67

article focuses on an intervention program aimed at families with handicapped children. Although these families may have unique problems, the lessons learned from them in designing interventions and developing methods for assessment and evaluation have potential transfer value to children and families in other areas of social work practice.

Parents of handicapped children face stressors that may exceed those of parenting a non-disabled child. Family members must cope with chronic and acute stressors when living with a child with developmental disabilities (Kazak, 1986; Shapiro, 1983). Researchers have documented such stressors as maladaptive and conflicting coping styles of the parents (Schilling, Schinke, & Kirkham, 1985), social isolation (Schilling & Schinke, 1984), chronic sorrow (Wikler, Wasow, & Hatfield, 1981), depression (Cummings, 1976), financial difficulties (Holroyd, 1974), and marital strain (Tew, Lawrence, Payne, & Rawnsley, 1977).

Interventions designed for parents of handicapped children have been primarily of three types: parent training designed to teach parents behavior management techniques for modifying the child's behavior; parent support groups designed to facilitate acceptance of the handicapped child; and advocacy groups developed to help parents find, develop, and participate in service programs available for their children. The common denominator in all these groups is the focus on managing the child's behavior or environment. Participants of these groups can share experiences with other parents of special needs children. However, sharing experiences alone may not result in skill gain or lasting improvement in parents' ability to cope with the handicapped child. The multitude of stressors faced by parents of handicapped children suggest that additional skills and services should be aimed specifically at their needs (Intagliata & Doyle, 1984; Schilling, 1988). Helping parents develop adaptive resources may enhance their sense of well-being which in turn has much to do with their ability to help the developmentally disabled child. Resources that parents and caregivers need include personal coping (McCubbin, Nevin, Cauble, Larsen, Comeau, & Patterson, 1982; Schilling, Gilchrist, & Schinke, 1984), social support (Kornblatt & Heinrich, 1985; Whittaker & Garbarino, 1983), environmental support (Eheart & Ciccone, 1982; Whittaker, 1986), and the integration of personal, social, and environmental resources (Schilling, 1988).

LIFE SKILLS TRAINING

A life skills training approach such as the one used in this study combines elements from traditional parent training programs with cognitive and behavioral training techniques. Life skills-building interventions can enhance individual coping through "providing cognitive and behavioral skills to help groups of people anticipate and cope with potential problems" (Gilchrist & Schinke, 1985). Typically included in life skills training are social and interpersonal communication techniques, problem solving, decision making, and conflict resolution techniques, and methods to affirm positive self-regard such as self-praise. Adapting the life skills training programs for parents of handicapped children the authors have added techniques to enable parents to develop and maintain a supportive social network and skills to enable the parents to advocate for services for themselves and their children.

Already used in programs to reduce stress in abusing families (Barth, Blythe, Schinke, & Schilling, 1983; Schilling & Kirkham, 1985) and to lower the risk of family violence (Schinke, Schilling, Barth, Gilchrist, & Maxwell, 1986), a life skills training program can be useful to families of handicapped children by teaching effective ways to cope, problem-solve, communicate, advocate for change, and develop social networks.

The life skills training program tested here is not just a skills-building program, but also a group program. Although skills-building approaches have been used with individuals, a group approach offers several advantages. Building cohesion and trust among group members can enhance treatment success (Rose, 1977). To enhance group cohesion several techniques were included in the training. Borrowing from earlier work with advocacy training for parents of handicapped children, an environmental change component was included in the treatment package. Each group chose a common problem in the community and directed their newly learned problem-solving techniques at the problem. Other techniques used to build group cohesion included using group members as peer leaders to demonstrate skills to each other, a buddy system was developed for reinforcement of the newly learned skills, group members were encouraged to meet outside the regularly scheduled sessions to work on the environmental change project, and a social support enhancement component was included in the training package. To enhance relevancy and increase members' investment in the training program, all the training examples came from the group members themselves. These and other elements of the program will be described in detail in the next section.

Structural issues were also considered by the investigators when designing the training program. Co-leadership was used in the skills-training groups to provide optimal ability of the group leaders to attend to content as well as process. One group leader was specifically responsible for the content of the session, while the other group leader took a supportive role helping the group stay on task, yet attending to process issues. To enhance the legitimacy of the group leaders at least one of the two group leaders was a parent of a child with a developmental disability. The other co-leader had been trained in cognitive-behavioral techniques. Group membership was also controlled by design. All group members were mothers of children with developmental disabilities. From the investigators' earlier research with families of handicapped children, there was evidence that too few fathers to obtain an adequate sample would participate in an intervention program. Therefore fathers were excluded from this research project to maintain a cleaner research design. In addition, there is some evidence to suggest that coping styles and social support network use may differ for fathers of handicapped children (Schilling, Schinke, & Kirkham, 1985). In light of these concerns, only mothers were invited to participate in the training programs.

DESIGN

This intervention evaluation study was designed to measure the effects of a life skills intervention and a traditional parent support group for mothers of handicapped children. Participants in this research study were mothers of children with a variety of developmental disabilities. Participants were recruited through Puget Sound area schools, mental health agencies, developmental preschools, and the Child Development and Mental Retardation Center at the

University of Washington. Mothers were randomly assigned to one of two treatment conditions: life skills intervention training or a traditional parent support group. Participants completed measurement instruments at pre and postintervention.

Subject Description

Over a two year period, 230 mothers of children with a variety of developmental disabilities participated in the research project. The following percentages are based on each mother's report of her child's primary disability: 19% mental retardation, 19% learning disabled, 13% neurological impairment, 13% language delay, 10% cerebral palsy, 6% epilepsy, 4% emotional disturbance, 4% hearing impairment, 4% autism, 2% visual impairment, and 6% other diagnoses. Approximately 75% of the children had more than one diagnosed impairment, and 55% had more than two diagnosed impairments. The children ranged in age from 2 to 14 years old, 62% were males, 21% had their disability diagnosed at birth while close to 30% weren't diagnosed until they were three years of age or older.

Mothers ranged in age from 22 to 69 years (34 years was the mean age). One mother was a grandmother providing the primary care for the child. The number of children in the families ranged from 1 to 9 (85% had 3 or fewer children). The majority of the participants (92%) were white, married (70%), and high school graduates (94%). Seventy-four percent had attended some college. Approximately half the families reported a yearly income of $20,000 or more.

Assessment

Participants were reimbursed for child care and mileage costs. Child care was provided on site at no cost to the participants throughout the assessment and training sessions. Refreshments were served and participants were paid $15 each time they completed the assessment battery.

Questionnaire on Resources and Stress (QRS-F)

This 52-item true-false instrument measures stress in families of handicapped children (Friedrich, Greenberg, & Crnic, 1983). The

QRS-F is divided into four subscales: Parent and Family Problem Scale assessing respondents' perceptions of problems for themselves or for their family; the Child Characteristics Scale assessing the degree of difficulty of their child's behavior; the Physical Incapacity Scale measuring the child's physical abilities, and a Pessimism Scale measuring respondents' beliefs about their child's future ability to achieve self-sufficiency. Kuder-Richardson 20 reliability coefficient for this measure is .95.

Beck Depression Inventory (BDI)

This 21-item instrument measures depression symptoms in respondents (Beck, Ward, Mendelson, Mock, & Erbaugh, 1961). Reliability of the BDI has been established at .93 (Beck & Beamesderfer, 1974).

Self-Reinforcement Attitudes Questionnaire (SRA)

A 20 question, four-point Likert type version of this self-report questionnaire measures the respondent's tendency toward self-reinforcement (Heiby, 1983). Test-retest and Spearman-Brown reliability have been established, respectively, at .92 and .87.

Inventory of Parent Experiences (IPE)

This 54-item measure assesses respondents' satisfaction with their social networks and general life situation (Crnic, Ragozin, Greenberg, & Robinson, 1981). Cronbach alpha reliability was .76. This measure was divided into six factors representing different aspects of the participant's social support network. The six factors included a measure of Parent Role Satisfaction which consists of items such as how satisfied the parent is with the number of people (professional and nonprofessional) she can turn to for help with a problem with her child, as well as satisfaction with time spent in child care duties; a Community Satisfaction factor consisting of items such as satisfaction with their involvement in their neighborhood and the number of organizations in their community; a Parent-Baby Pleasure factor which consists of items assessing satisfaction with child care duties; a Friendship Satisfaction factor measuring participants' satisfaction with their existing friendship networks; a

Family Satisfaction factor consisting of items related to participants' satisfaction with contact and help from parents and relatives; and a Relationship Satisfaction Scale that consists of items to assess the participants' satisfaction with intimate relationships.

Communication

In written response to vignettes and knowledge questions, mothers demonstrated their skill in using the communication skills taught in class. Interrater and intrarater reliability for this measure was established at .86.

DESCRIPTION OF INTERVENTIONS

Life Skills Training

Two social workers co-led the groups twice a week for nine 2-hour sessions. Through discussion, modeling, rehearsal, and homework assignments, parents learned personal coping strategies, practiced communication skills, applied a problem-solving model as individuals to problems relevant to their respective families and as a group to problems in the community shared by group members, and developed their social support networks (Kirkham, Norelius, Meltzer, Schilling, & Schinke, 1988).

Coping Skills Training

Following introductions of participants the training session focused on group discussion of the difficulties parents face when raising a child with special needs. Drawing on participants' experiences, group leaders helped them identify their own thoughts and internal statements that could influence the stress or perceived threat of a given situation. Additional coping statements were introduced by group leaders. Parents then developed lists of personal coping strategies including self-praise statements, reminders of their child's positive characteristics, and future relief times. A homework assignment stressed practice using these positive messages at home.

Interpersonal Communication

Interpersonal communication skills were taught to help parents build social support networks and advocate for their children in the community. Group members systematically practiced listening skills, nonverbal cues, and strategies to handle criticism. They identified ways to initiate contacts via telephone, accept and express appreciation, and request and offer help to others. Participants discussed ways to introduce the sensitive topic of a child's handicap, and how to assess and interpret others' verbal and nonverbal responses.

Problem-solving

Parents were taught a problem-solving model as another facet of personal coping. In class, the group collectively solved several problems they had previously identified. In groups of two or three, participants practiced applying the problem-solving model to problems they or their families were currently experiencing. Parents signed contracts with classmates to support home efforts to apply the problem-solving process to a frequently occurring problem.

Environmental Change Project

As part of the training program, participants were directed to collectively apply the problem-solving model to make favorable changes in the larger environment. Parents suggested and considered possible targets of change in the community or neighborhood. After a specific goal was identified by the group, leaders helped parents develop a plan for implementing the change. Tasks were broken down into manageable steps, and the completion of tasks was shared by group members as homework assignments. Parents reported on their progress at subsequent sessions. Environmental change projects included developing a speakers bureau where professionals in the community presented their agencies' programs to parents of handicapped children; brochures with information for friends and relatives of families with handicapped children, an assessment tool to determine children's developmental stages, and resource lists with information on recreational and child care programs for handicapped children.

Social Support Enhancement

The social support component of the training focused on teaching parents ways to identify different levels of social support, from intimate friends to acquaintances; how to initiate conversations and maintain contacts, and how to identify the type of support they received from each person. Using special homework forms, they practiced ways to balance their social networks by increasing positive relationships and decreasing negative contacts.

One of the advantages of groups is the opportunity for mutual support. As parents developed individual plans for changing their social networks they contracted with a "buddy" in the group. Buddies offered alternative solutions and encouragement as parents carried out their plans.

The final session reviewed the concepts presented in the course and emphasized the skills parents identified as the most difficult. Parents also reported on their plans for collectively acting to improve conditions for handicapped children and their families.

Comparison Group Intervention

Parents assigned to the comparison treatment condition participated in a parent support group led by a social worker affiliated with the University of Washington School of Social Work. The groups met over the intervention period to explore family relationships and examine the advantages and disadvantages of working with professionals. Group activities involved discussion, sharing of resources, and mutual support among the participants. Mothers contributed to a community bulletin board, and shared a favorite book on disabilities with the group. The groups also hosted a guest speaker who spoke of her personal experiences growing up with a disability. Although both types of groups had similar aims (i.e., mutual support, sharing of resources, etc.), a specific focus on skill training was not included in the parent support group.

RESULTS

Training programs were conducted in the Spring and Fall of the two project years. A total of 230 participants attended 21 separate training groups. Chi-square analyses revealed no significant differences between groups on demographic data. All groups for each condition were combined for the posttreatment analyses.

An overall MANOVA was performed on the pretest scores of the regrouped data revealing no significant differences between mean vectors of the two treatment groups. Tables 1 and 2 list group means and standard deviations for all outcome variables at pre and immediate posttest, respectively. Examination of Table 1 reveals

Table 1.   Pretest Scores on Outcome Variables

| | Group | | | |
| | Experimental n = 143 | | Comparison n = 72 | |
Measures	M	SD	M	SD
Beck Depression Inventory	9.17	7.59	9.29	7.84
Self Reinforcement Attitude*	2.21	.34	2.15	.32
Inventory of Parent Experiences				
Parent-role satisfaction	15.86	3.45	16.08	3.41
Community satisfaction	5.26	1.31	5.54	1.45
Parent-baby pleasure	11.13	2.09	10.86	2.06
Friendship satisfaction	11.23	2.78	12.03	2.45
Family satisfaction	11.34	2.99	11.50	2.97
Relationship satisfaction	12.58	3.38	13.61	2.72
Questionnaire on Resources & Stress				
Parent family problems	39.54	26.78	37.08	25.81
Pessimism	30.64	15.48	31.17	25.09
Physical incapacitation	12.49	12.57	12.24	12.30
Child characteristics	36.70	16.99	39.49	17.96
Communication skills	4.04	2.68	3.75	2.86

* Average scores (total score/number of items responded).   A low score on this measure indicates high degree of self reinforcement.

Table 2. Posttest Scores on Outcome Variables

	Group			
	Experimental		Comparison	
	n = 143		n = 72	
Measures	M	SD	M	SD
Beck Depression Inventory	6.59	5.80	7.83	6.97
Self Reinforcement Attitude*	1.98	.35	2.12	.33
Inventory of Parent Experiences				
Parent-role satisfaction	17.30	3.58	16.98	3.80
Community satisfaction	5.54	1.48	5.65	1.29
Parent-baby pleasure	11.79	2.15	11.12	1.84
Friendship satisfaction	12.23	2.78	12.41	2.63
Family satisfaction	11.78	2.96	11.14	2.93
Relationship satisfaction	13.28	3.12	12.36	2.90
Questionnaire on Resources & Stress				
Parent family problems	32.15	25.71	34.49	25.15
Pessimism	27.99	17.12	28.88	17.96
Physical incapacitation	10.48	12.21	12.14	12.41
Child characteristics	33.81	18.16	38.68	18.16
Communication skills	7.83	2.31	4.71	2.79

* Average scores (total score/number of items responded). A low score on this measure indicates high degree of self reinforcement.

that the comparison treatment group scores were better on eight of the thirteen outcome variables (although not significantly) at pretest than the experimental group's scores. Nevertheless to control for any initial differences between individuals, pretest scores were entered as covariates in the outcome analyses. Plotting the distribution of the residuals revealed that the data (with the exception of the Physical Incapacitation Scale) followed a normal distribution. Plotting the residuals against the predicted values supported the assumption of a constant variance.

Following the pattern of responses on the Physical Incapacitation Scale, scores were recoded into the following groups: those with a zero stress score indicating no stress on this scale, those whose scores range within 5 to 15 points, and those whose scores ranged from 16 to 36 points. Chi-square analysis was performed on this measure rather than the multiple regression analysis approach applied to the other outcome variables because of the nonnormal distribution of the scores on the Physical Incapacitation Scale.

Multiple regression analyses were performed on posttreatment scores for all participants. Initially each posttreatment variable's corresponding pretest score and demographic variables that were conceptually relevant were entered into the equation. Demographic variables included marital status, age of parent, age of child, sex of child, income, and level of disability of the child. Mothers' perceptions of the severity of their children's disabilities (mild, moderate, severe) were dummy coded into two dichotomous variables and entered into the equation (Kleinbaum & Kupper, 1978). Variables not contributing significantly to the explained variance were dropped and the models refitted using only those variables that contributed significantly to the total explained variance in outcome scores. In all cases, treatment group was entered last. Treatment condition was coded 1 for experimental group and 0 for comparison treatment group. In most cases, only the pretest score and treatment group were significant predictors of outcome. Age of the child, and severity of the child's condition entered some models and will be noted below. In the presentation that follows, the total variance and the significance level of the group effect will be reported. See Table 3 for a listing of R^2 changes and significance level for each independent variable. Power of the posttest analyses ranged from .50 for determining a small effect size to greater than .98 for determining a medium to large effect size (Cohen, 1977). The following sections summarize the findings for each measure at the immediate posttreatment assessment.

Personal Coping

Multiple regression analysis revealed that mothers who participated in the skills-building group improved on the Self-Reinforcement Attitude Survey more than the comparison treatment group when controlling for pretest scores ($R^2 = .406$, $p < .001$). Examination of Tables 1 and 2 reveal that the comparison treatment group made almost no movement in their ability to use self-reinforcement.

Table 3. Results of Multiple Regression Analysis on Posttest variables. Overall R^2 and R^2 change for each variable

Outcome variable	Total R^2	Prescore	Independent Variables (R^2 change)		
			Treatment Group	Child's Age	Perception of Disability
Beck Depression Inventory	.451	.442*	.008***		
Self-Reinforcement Attitude Survey	.406	.353*	.052*		
Communication Skills	.413	.127*	.285*		
Stress					
Parent-Family Factor	.726	.721*	.004***		
Pessimism	.646	.646*	.000		
Child Characteristics	.700	.681*	.002		.016**
Social Support					
Parent-Role Satisfaction	.469	.467*	.002		
Parent-Baby Pleasure	.421	.412*	.009***		
Friendship Satisfaction	.349	.322*	.001	.025**	
Relationship Satisfaction	.578	.568*	.009**		
Family Satisfaction	.577	.564*	.013**	.013***	
Community Satisfaction	.270	.256*	.000		

* p < .001
** p < .05
*** p < .10

79

Communication Skills

Changes in the communication skill measure indicated that mothers in the skills-building group showed significant improvement in their use of communication skills when controlling for pretest score ($R^2 = .413, p < .001$).

Depression

Mothers in the experimental treatment group reported a greater reduction in depression levels at posttest than mothers in the comparison treatment group ($R^2 = .451, p <. 08$).

Social Support Satisfaction

On the subscales that related to family relationships, mothers in the skills-building group reported significantly higher levels of use and satisfaction with family support and intimate relationship support as measured by the Family Satisfaction Scale ($R^2 = .577, p < .05$) and the Relationship Satisfaction Scale ($R^2 = .568, p < .05$) respectively. In addition, the experimental treatment group's level of satisfaction of child caregiving duties was greater (at statistical significance level of $p < .09$) at posttest than the comparison treatment group as measured by the Parent-Baby Pleasure Scale ($R^2 = .421, p < .09$).

On the measures of social support that dealt with relationships outside the family (Friendship Satisfaction, Community Satisfaction, and Parent-Role Satisfaction), the experimental group made larger gains (albeit not statistically significant) in the desired direction. Mothers of older children demonstrated greater improvement in their satisfaction level with friendships ($p < .05$) and with their community ($p < .06$).

Stress

Multiple regression analysis revealed that participants in the skills-building group reported larger gains in reducing their level of stress on the Parent and Family Problem Scale ($R^2 = .72, p < .08$). On the two remaining measures of stress (Pessimism and Child

Characteristic Scales), the skills-building group made greater movement in the desired direction than the comparison treatment group although not statistically significant. Mothers of severely disabled children reported higher levels of stress as measured by the Child Characteristics Scale ($p < .05$).

Chi-square analysis of posttest scores revealed no significant differences between groups on the Physical Incapacitation Scale X^2 (2, $N = 215$) = $1.32, p > .51$.

Summary of Posttest Analyses

In summary, at assessment immediately posttreatment, mothers who participated in the skills-building treatment condition reported significantly larger gains in coping skills as measured by the Self-Reinforcement Attitude Survey; in communication skill level; in satisfaction with family support as measured by Family Satisfaction and Relationship Satisfaction Scales; and near significant reduction in depression and stress levels.

Mothers of severely disabled children reported a higher level of stress as measured by the Child Characteristics Scale. Mothers of older children reported greater satisfaction with community social supports as measured by the Friendship Satisfaction and Community Satisfaction Scale.

DISCUSSION

The literature on families with handicapped children suggests that the problems these families experience may be related more to the coping and support resources available to them than to the physical or mental condition of the children (Schilling, Schinke, & Kirkham, 1988; Zeitlin, Williamson, & Rosenblatt, 1987). Designed to teach parents ways to develop and enhance their coping and social support resources, the results of this evaluation study shows promise for a life skills development focus rather than a more traditional parent support group.

Communication and Coping Skills

One of the main focuses of the skills training model was to improve coping resources for parents. Included as coping resources were problem solving ability, communication skill, and cognitive appraisal. The outcome of the measurement of both communication and coping skills demonstrates that participants in the life skills training program were able to improve their skills over an 8-week period. Homework assignments and products from the group projects provided evidence that participants were able to utilize the problem-solving model in both individual and group situations.

Family Relationships

The measures on stress and social support satisfaction give consistent results regarding the impact of the intervention on improving family relationships at posttest. The skills-building group reported greater satisfaction with family relationships and reduced stress relating to family interactions. The majority of the exercises and examples presented in the intervention model focused on improving family relationships with a particular emphasis on the mother's relationship with the handicapped child. This emphasis may explain why family relationships and not relationships outside the family showed any improvement.

As with communication and coping skills, the mother's relationship with the handicapped child was addressed in the first three sessions of the training. In addition, the coping skills related specifically to coping with the handicapped child. Identifying and making changes in other relationships (although focused mostly on the family) was not addressed until the seventh and eighth session. Perhaps participants did not have enough opportunity to practice the skills presented in the last sessions so maintenance and generalization to other settings was difficult to achieve.

Child's Age

Mothers of older children also reported greater satisfaction with their friendships and the community at posttest. Wilton and Renant (1986) found that stress levels are higher in mothers of younger children. Mothers of older children have likely had more time to adjust to the fact of the disability and mobilize friends and families. This may be a function of the length of time these families have lived in the community. Mothers of older children may have been in the community longer providing for more time to establish friendships and become familiar with services in the community.

DIRECTIONS FOR RESEARCH

Although the results lend support for a life skills training approach to improving the functioning of families with handicapped children several issues remain to be addressed in further research. Some of those issues outlined here include the representativeness of the sample, the influence of the child's disability, the types of problems chosen as the focus of training and practice, the opportunity for practice of each skill, and the impact of group process.

Sample Selection

One concern researchers and practitioners may have regarding this research design is the choice of subjects. Participants were parents, who from the outset, were seeking services for themselves. Some parents were willing to drive over 100 miles each session to participate. These participants volunteered to attend the sessions which suggests that they may have their lives sufficiently organized so that they are able to participate in a parent training program. The scores on the Beck Depression Inventory indicated that the majority of the participants were not depressed at pretest. This contradicts findings of other studies on mothers of handicapped children. The outcome may be very different for isolated parents already having difficulty coping. The skills training may not be as effective for depressed individuals.

Disability

Participants in this study were parents of children with a wide range of disabilities. As discussed earlier, severity of disability may be affecting outcome but the impact of the disability cannot be sufficiently isolated in this study. Actual diagnosis was not found to predict outcome. A confounding factor is that over 75% of the children had more than one disability. Matching or controlling for disability would have resulted in sample sizes too small to detect a treatment effect.

The level of the child's disability may also affect mothers' ability to benefit from a life skills training program. Caregiving responsibilities can drain the parent of energy and time necessary for participating in interventions aimed at enhancing parents' functioning. The impact of the disability on mothers' coping is suggested by a study on maternal distress. In a path analysis of factors relating to maternal distress and coping, Breslau (1983) found that the disability of the child relates indirectly to maternal distress through affecting the family repertoire of activities which in turn affects the mother's sense of self-efficacy. Further research should control for developmental age of the child, the amount of care each participant provides for the child, and the extent to which child's age and condition affect parents' ability to assimilate and use training content.

Component Analysis

Of interest to researchers and practitioners is the effectiveness of the intervention as a package as well as the effectiveness of each of its components. The present study was evaluated as a treatment package. Evaluation of each component as a separate intervention could suggest a variety implementation models in which all or parts of the model presented here could be combined.

Opportunity for Practice

The results of this study suggest that opportunity for practice may affect immediate outcome. The skills that showed the greatest improvement were those placed earlier in the training program subsequently providing for the greatest opportunity for practice. Manipulation of the placement of the skills, the number of rehearsals, and the use of training approaches (role play, modeling, etc.) may also provide valuable information on what is needed to achieve proficiency.

Group Effects

A final concern is the influence of the use of group on the training outcome. Although skills training approaches have been used with individuals it is doubtful that this program would have been as effective when used as an individual approach—particularly the social support and environmental change aspect of the training. Further research should attempt to control for some group effects by making them a variable in the study. For example, in the current study it is assumed that group cohesion was enhanced in the skills training group, but the extent of group cohesiveness, sense of purpose, and group identity was not measured in either group. The impact of group process issues must be controlled for in future studies.

CONCLUSION

A two-year study aimed at testing a group intervention designed to enhance coping, communication, and problem-solving skills, and social support networks of mothers of handicapped children was implemented and evaluated with 230 participants. Multiple regression analyses revealed that participants in the life skills-building group improved their self-reinforcement ability and satisfaction with their social networks, and reduced their stress levels significantly more than mothers who participated in a traditional parent support group. Further research should focus on the impact of family functioning and group process on skills-building intervention outcomes.

REFERENCES

Barth, R.P., Blythe, B. J., Schinke, S.P., & Schilling, R. F. (1983). Self control training for maltreating parents. *Child Welfare*, *62*, 314-324.

Beck, A. T., & Beamesderfer, A. (1974). Assessment of depression: The Depression Inventory. In P. Pichot & R. Olivier-Martin (Eds.), *Psychological measurements in psychopharmacology* (pp. 151-169). Basel, Switzerland: J. Karger.

Beck, A. T., Ward, C. H., Mendelson, M., Mock, J., & Erbaugh, J. (1961). An inventory of measuring depression. *Archives of General Psychiatry*, *4*, 561-571.

Breslau, N. (1983). Family care: Effects on siblings and mothers. In G. H. Thompson, I. L. Rubin, & R. M. Bilenker (Eds.), *Comprehensive management of cerebral palsy* (pp. 299-309). New York: Grune & Stratton.

Cohen, J. (1977). *Statistical power analysis for the behavioral sciences*. Orlando: Academic Press.

Crnic, K., Ragozin, A., Greenberg, M., & Robinson, N. (1981). *Inventory of parents' experiences*. University of Washington, Seattle, WA.

Cummings, S. T. (1976). The impact of the child's deficiency on the father: A study of fathers of mentally retarded and of chronically ill children. *American Journal of Orthopsychiatry, 46*, 246-255.

Eheart, E. & Ciccone, J. (1982). Special needs of low-income mothers of developmentally delayed children. *American Journal of Mental Deficiency, 87*, 26-33.

Friedrich W. N., Greenberg M. T., & Crnic K. A. (1983). A short-form of the questionnaire on resources and stress. *American Journal of Mental Deficiency, 88*, 41-48.

Gilchrist, L. D., & Schinke, S. P. (1985). Prevention of social and health problems. In L.D. Gilchrist & S. P. Schinke (Eds.), *Prevention of social and health problems through life-skills training* (Center for Social Welfare Research Monograph No. 3; pp. 11-14). Seattle: University of Washington Press.

Hartman, A. (1981). The family: A central focus for practice. *Social Work, 26*, 7-15.

Heiby, E. B. (1983). Assessment of frequency of self-reinforcement. *Journal of Personality and Social Psychology, 44*, 1304-1307.

Holroyd, J. (1974). The questionnaire on resources and stress: An instrument to measure family response to a handicapped family member. *Journal of Community Psychology, 2*, 92-94.

Intagliata, J., & Doyle, N. (1984). Enhancing social support for parents of developmentally disabled children: Training in interpersonal problem solving skills. *Mental Retardation, 22*, 4-11.

Kazak, A. E. (1986). Families with physically handicapped children: Social ecology and family systems. *Family Process, 25*, 265-281.

Kirkham, M.A., Norelius, K. L., Meltzer, N. J., Schilling, R. F., & Schinke, S. P. (1988). *Reducing stress in mothers of disabled children*. Seattle: University of Washington Press.

Kleinbaum, D. G., & Kupper. L. L. (1978). *Applied regression analysis and other multivariable methods*. Boston: Duxbury.

Kornblatt, E. S., & Heinrich, J. (1985). Needs and coping abilities in families of children with developmental disabilities. *Mental Retardation, 23*, 13-20.

McCubbin, H. I., Nevin, R. S., Cauble, A. E., Larsen, A., Comeau, J.K., & Patterson, J. M. (1982). Family coping with chronic illness: The case of cerebral palsy. In H. I. McCubbin, A. E. Cauble, & J. M. Patterson, *Family stress, coping, and social support* (pp.169-188). Springfield, IL: Charles C Thomas.

Rose, S. D. (1977). *Group therapy: A behavioral approach*. Englewood Cliffs, NJ: Prentice Hall.

Schilling, R. F. (1988). Helping families with developmentally disabled members. In C. Chilman, F. Cox, & E. Nunnally (Eds.), *Troubled families: Vol. 2. Chronic illness and disability* (pp. 171-192). Beverly Hills: Sage.

Schilling, R. F., Gilchrist, L. D., & Schinke, S. P. (1984). Coping and social support in families of developmentally disabled children. *Family Relations*, *33*, 47-54.

Schilling, R. F., & Kirkham, M. A. (1985). Preventing maltreatment of handicapped children. In L. D. Gilchrist & S. P. Schinke, (Eds.), *Preventing social and health problems through life skills training* (Center for Social Welfare Research Monograph No. 3; pp.29-42). Seattle: University of Washington Press.

Schilling, R. F., & Schinke, S. P. (1984). Personal coping and social support for parents of handicapped children. *Children and Youth Services Review*, *6*, 195-206.

Schilling, R. F., Schinke, S. P., & Kirkham, M. A. (1985). Coping with a handicapped child: Differences between mothers and fathers. *Social Science and Medicine*, *21*, 857-863.

Schilling, R. F., Schinke, S. P., & Kirkham, M. A. (1988). The impact of developmental disabilities and other learning deficits on families. In C. Chilman, F. Cox, & E. Nunnally (Eds.), *Troubled families: Vol. 2. Chronic illness and disability* (pp. 156-170). Beverly Hills: Sage.

Schinke, S. P., Schilling, R. F., Barth, R. P., Gilchrist, L. D., & Maxwell, J. S. (1986). Stress management intervention to prevent family violence. *Journal of Family Violence*, *1*, 13-26.

Shapiro, J. (1983). Family reactions and coping strategies in response to the physically ill or handicapped child: A review. *Social Science and Medicine*, *17*, 913-931.

Tew, B. J., Lawrence, K. M., Payne, H., & Rawnsley, K. (1977). Marital stability following the birth of a child with spina bifida. *British Journal of Preventive and Social Medicine*, *29*, 27-30.

Whittaker, J. K. (1986). Formal and informal helping in child welfare services: Implications for management and practice. *Child Welfare*, *65*, 17-25.

Whittaker, J. K., Garbarino, J., & Associates (1983). *Social support networks: informal helping in the human services*. New York: Aldine.

Wikler, L., Wasow, M., & Hatfield, E. (1981). Chronic sorrow revisited: Parent vs. professional depiction of the adjustment of parents of mentally retarded children. *American Journal of Orthopsychiatry*, *51*, 63-70.

Wilton, K., & Renaut, J. (1986). Stress levels in families with intellectually handicapped preschool children and families with nonhandicapped preschool children. *Journal of Mental Deficiency*, *90*, 703-706.

Zeitlin, S., Williamson, G. G., & Rosenblatt, W. P. (1987). The coping with stress model: A counseling approach for families with a handicapped child. *Journal of Counseling and Development*, *65*, 443-446.

The Effect of Process
and Structured Content on Outcome
in Stress Management Groups

Dale Whitney
Sheldon D. Rose

SUMMARY. This study of stress management via group therapy evaluated the effect of group process and structured content on the reduction of stress. Group process focused mainly on cohesion, interpersonal learning, self-disclosure, and group norms. Structured content consisted of relaxation training, assertiveness training, and cognitive restructuring. Sixty-four subjects were randomly assigned to four conditions: (1) Group Process, (2) High Structure, (3) Combined (process and structure), and (4) Control (waiting list). Results showed that the 3 treatment conditions (1-3) were significantly better than no treatment on at least one dependent measure, and although not statistically significant, the conditions enhancing group process (1 and 3 above) were generally superior to those that didn't.

INTRODUCTION

The popularity of stress management groups in clinical practice and occupational settings comes as no surprise in view of the regularity of stress in most peoples' everyday lives. While there has been a plethora of research on the effectiveness of various ap-

---

Dale Whitney, PhD, is Director of Behavioral Sciences in the family practice clinic at Scott Airforce Base, Bellville, IL. Sheldon D. Rose, PhD, is Professor, School of Social Work, University of Wisconsin, Madison, WI 53706.

This study was partially supported by a grant from the Wisconsin Alumni Research Foundation. Correspondence should be directed to Sheldon D. Rose, School of Social Work, 425 Henry Mall, University of Wisconsin, Madison, WI 53706.

89

proaches to stress management in such groups (e.g., Foreman, 1981; Tisdelle, Hansen, St. Lawrence, Kelly, & Brown, 1982; Kelly, Bradlyn, Dubbert, & St. Lawrence, 1983; Tallant, Rose, & Tolman, in press; Tolman & Rose, in press) a review of outcome research on group treatment (Rose, Tolman, & Tallant, 1986) revealed that almost none of these studies even considered the issue of group *process*, much less how it affects outcome in group treatment. Yet practitioners assert that group process variables are extremely important for change in group therapy. For this reason a study was developed in which a structured program and some elements of group process are examined in terms of their separate and combined impact on stress reduction in stress management groups. Both the structured elements (content) and the group process elements that were manipulated are now described as they were conceptualized and operationalized in this study. Each of these will be initially defined from the perspective of an ideal model developed in previous studies (see Tolman & Rose, in press; Tallant, Rose, & Tolman, in press) which combines both structure and process.

STRUCTURED CONTENT
OF STRESS MANAGEMENT TRAINING

The structured content selected for study can be described within three general sets of procedures embedded in a systematic problem solving paradigm. These elements are (1) relaxation training, (2) cognitive restructuring, and (3) a modeling sequence to teach assertive techniques and other social skills. Let us examine briefly each of these elements, and the way they were put together in a treatment package.

Relaxation Training

In contrast to the frequently undesirable physical and emotional responses to stress, such as tense muscles and feelings of anxiety, relaxation can be used as an alternative response to aid in coping both during and subsequent to a stressful situation. It can be used as a general life-style skill which may, in itself, contribute to stress reduction. However, most persons can not effectively relax without some training. The training method used in this study utilized progressive muscular techniques as described by Bernstein and Borkovec (1973). This approach calls for guiding participants through a series of exercises in which various muscles throughout the body are intentionally contracted ("tensed") and released ("let go"), which leads to feelings of pleasure and relaxation as the person lets go of the "tension." Deep breathing and imagery (e.g., the person imagines being in a pleasant, relaxing environment, such as alone on the beach) are also taught to further enhance relaxation.

Cognitive Restructuring

Many persons with high levels of stress deal with stress-inducing situations with faulty assumptions and negative self-talk (e.g., "I'll never be able to do that" or "I'm sure they won't like me"). Cognitive restructuring is a set of procedures used to demonstrate and train in positive thinking, positive self-talk, and correcting faulty beliefs in the face of stressors (many of these procedures are developments of the work of Meichenbaum, 1977 and Beck, 1976).

This set of procedures was adapted to group stress programs to help participants replace negative cognitions with positive ones. Exercises were designed to help participants *recognize* negative self-talk and "automatic" thoughts, and transform them into positive self-talk. Self-defeating statements were likewise changed into self-enhancing statements. Cognitive modeling and rehearsals were also an important part of teaching these skills.

Modeling Sequence

As adapted to this study, this set of procedures included: (1) situational analysis (evaluation of feelings, objectives, and probable consequences in a given situation), (2) modeling (the leader or another group member demonstrates the given social skill), (3) behavioral rehearsal (the person practices the skill in front of the group), (4) coaching (the leader or another group member gives suggestions and encouragement as the skill is being practiced), and (5) feedback (the leader and other group members praise what is done well and recommend what might be done differently). The theoretical foundation for this sequence is expostulated in Bandura (1977).

The modeling sequence was used to help clients deal more effectively with day-to-day situations involving interpersonal stress. In addition, by means of the sequence, specific assertive techniques were taught such as assertive refusal (saying "No!"), making assertive requests, openly expressing feelings, giving and receiving positive and negative feedback (e.g., praise and criticism), negative assertion (admitting mistakes), and "anger starvation" (letting the other person express anger without getting angry or defensive in return).

Having described each of the three components of structure, let us examine how they are tied together in a general problem-solving paradigm.

Systematic Problem-Solving

The structural aspect of the stress management training model includes formal teaching and experiential practice in all three components described above. This is facilitated by clients bringing in their own specific stress-inducing situations, and learning, through systematic problem-solving, to analyze these situations (which includes identifying stressors in their lives and identifying their inappropriate coping responses). Then, with the help of the group they generate and later evaluate potential alternative coping strategies as they can be applied to their individual stress-inducing situations. Each member then selects the strategies they wish to employ and these are demonstrated and practiced in the group. Finally they try out these coping strategies in the real world and report back to the group how these strategies worked. These are the major steps of systematic problem solving (see Heppner, 1981, for a more complete discussion of the assumptions and research related to systematic problem solving).

These structural elements occur within the context of a group. Whether or not it is the intention of the leader, group processes are generated, which are likely to impinge on outcome. In the following section, we shall clarify how processes are identified and dealt with in this model.

GROUP PROCESS
IN STRESS MANAGEMENT TRAINING

There are many possible elements of group process. Most seem to be interrelated. For example group cohesion seems to be related to self-disclosure, broad distribution of participation, and positive attitudes toward the leader and the group. Although they appear interrelated, no one has demonstrated a causal relationship of one element or attribute to the others. If they are, in fact, interrelated, it should be possible to influence any one of them, and get a corresponding effect on the others.

As noted above, one particular variable in group therapy that seems closely related to cohesion, and can be readily influenced by a leader is the degree of participation or involvement of the members. If the leader involves the members by asking for their opinions and experiences, by letting them answer each other's questions, and by involving them in group exercises, this should influence or result in broad participation. If our assumption is correct about the interrelatedness of group process elements, broad participation and involvement should result in greater cohesion, increased self-disclosure, less escape behavior, and ultimately better outcomes. Since participation seemed the most readily modified aspect of group process, it is the central concept utilized or the central process element manipulated in this study. Although not manipulated in this study, one other concept, group cohesion, is examined as it might impinge on group process.

Group cohesion is a concept that is defined differentially by scholars in the field (e.g., Stokes, 1983; Yalom, 1985, and Lott & Lott, 1965). We have elected to define it as "the mutual attraction of the group's members to each other," because such a definition is readily operationalized, and it covers the significant theoretical aspects of the concept.

Purpose of Study

The major question that this study is asking is whether or not group process in general, and broad involvement of members in particular, makes any difference in terms of outcome. A more specific purpose of this study is to determine the impact of broad client involvement/participation and the impact of structured content on outcome in stress management groups. Since broad involvement is assumed to influence the other elements of group process in a pro-therapeutic way, we would expect support for the following hypothesis: Stress management training groups which have a high level of structured content *and* a high level of member involvement will be more effective in reducing stress than groups in which there is a preponderance of either structure or involvement almost to the exclusion of the other.

We would also hypothesize that groups in which involvement of members is low will result in less reduction in stress than those in which involvement is high. In terms of the conditions of this study, it was expected that clients in the treatment conditions with high involvement plus stress management training (Combined Condition) and the clients in the High Involvement Condition only would more effectively reduce stress as compared to the High Structure (low involvement plus stress management training) groups and the Wait List controls.

Finally, we would hypothesize that subjects in groups receiving stress management training will show greater reduction of stress than those not receiving such treatment.

METHOD

Recruitment of Subjects

In order to test the above hypotheses a before-after design with control and contrast groups to which clients are randomly assigned was selected. Sufficient number of subjects were believed to be available to use such a design. Experience with a previous study (Tallant, Rose, & Tolman, in press) suggested that 64 persons would provide sufficient power to reject the null hypotheses. Thus, 64 subjects were recruited from the general population of a medium sized midwestern community, by placing posters in public agencies, and by placing ads in newspapers. Local radio stations and a public television station also ran announcements.

Subjects were initially screened on the telephone at which time the stress management groups and the nature of the study was explained. They were then given an individual appointment for: (1) completion of demographic information, (2) an assessment of current problems, symptoms, and treatment goals, (3) administration of the dependent measures of stress, and (4) a review of the conditions and requirements of the study.

Assignment of Subjects

After initial assessment, subjects were randomly assigned to one of four conditions. The first condition encouraged member involvement to the maximum extent possible, but only limited structure was provided. There was no formal teaching, and information on relaxation, cognitive restructuring, and the modeling sequence was not provided. Leader involvement was minimized, especially avoiding answering technical questions calling for factual information. The central focus was on intermember discussion of personal situations and stress-related problems. This represented a "High Involvement" Condition.

In the second condition, intermember involvement was not encouraged in any explicit way in favor of a highly structured situation where teaching and learning information was the emphasis in a "classroom" kind of atmosphere. Almost all of the interaction was between the leader and a member rather than between the members themselves. This represented the "High Structure" Condition.

The Combined Condition used all the structural elements (minilectures, specific training in relaxation, cognitive restructuring, and the modeling sequence) but at the same time encouraged input by members through involving them in the discussion to answer questions, bring in their own specific problems, provide ideas for each other, etc. It should be noted that even though the Combined Condition was characterized by both "high" structure and "high" involvement, that relatively speaking, the Combined Condition was less structured than the High Structured Condition and provided less involvement than the High Involvement Condition. (For all three conditions treatment manuals are available on request from the second author.)

Finally, the fourth condition was the Wait List Control group. No structure was provided, and there was no member involvement in this group as these subjects attended no sessions and/or did not meet as a group at any time during the study.

Once assigned to a condition, subjects were randomly assigned to one of two groups *within* each condition. There were originally eight subjects in each of the six treatment groups, and 20 subjects in the Wait List Control Condition group for a total of 68 in the sample. However, after notification of assignment to groups, several subjects withdrew from the study due to schedule conflicts and discontent over being placed in the Wait List Control Condition group (even though they had initially agreed to "take their chances"). However, since subjects with low scores as measured by the dependent measures would have little room for improvement and consequently would be unable to show treatment effects, they were excluded from analysis (but allowed to remain in their assigned groups, and attend all sessions). Once these low scores were excluded, there were no significant differences between conditions before treatment.

Also, after elimination of low scores, the final size of the population to be considered in the study consisted of 11 in the High Involvement Condition, 15 in the High Structure Condition, 14 in the Combined Condition, and 14 in the Wait List Control group.

Subjects in the three treatment conditions (High Involvement, High Structure, and Combined) participated in a two-hour group session once per week for nine weeks. There were two leaders both with extensive experience and training in leading groups. Each leader was randomly assigned to one of the two groups in each of the three treatment conditions.

Dependent Measures

Dependent measures included the Daily Hassles Scale to focus on perceived stress from environmental stressors, (Lazarus, 1981), the Profile of Mood States to determine the extent of stress manifested through mood disturbances (Derogatis, 1977), the SCL-90-R to determine the level of stress manifested by physical symptoms (McNair, Lorr, & Droppelman, 1971).

Measures were first administered in individual pre-treatment interviews (before treatment), again after the ninth group session (after treatment), and a third time 2 months after group sessions had ended (follow-up). However, for ethical reasons, follow-up measures for the Wait List Control group were not administered, in that subjects in this group were offered treatment immediately following the ninth session.

Posttests were administered to subjects in the treatment conditions during the last group session. They were administered to the subjects in the Wait List Condition by means of mailing the dependent measures to them, after which they were returned by mail. Unfortunately, only 9 of the 14 subjects in the Wait List group completed and returned the posttest measures. This may have had a significant impact on the results reported below. Follow-up measures for all treatment subjects were also administered by mail.

Independent Variables

Measures used to evaluate the degree of success in manipulating the independent variables included a post *session* questionnaire (completed at the end of each session), an observer to record participation data in each session, and an audio recording of every session. The post session questionnaire (Rose & Brower, 1986) provided information on group cohesion, perception of involvement, and perception of degree of self and other self-disclosure.

Participation data was collected by an observer who recorded, at ten second intervals, which person in the group was talking/participating. The observer also recorded whether the discussion was: (1) between two members, (2) between a leader and a member, or (3) whether the discussion was from either the leader or a member, and was directed to the entire group rather than anyone in particular. The observers also coded the degree to which each person self-disclosed at each session on a five-point scale.

Audio recordings were made of each session to permit analysis and differentiation of conditions based only on *what* people said and *how* they said it. An independent research assistant who, after getting briefed on the characteristics and objectives of each condition, attempted to determine which tapes were from which treatment condition. This assistant knew nothing else about the study, yet was able to differentiate many of the tapes according to condition (even though listening only to random segments).

RESULTS

Manipulation Checks

In reviewing the results from the participation data, support was provided that the manipulation of the independent variables was successful (see Table 1).

The differences between groups in terms of the direction of discussion was significant ($p < .01$). As was predicted if the manipulation was successful, there was more member to group discussion in the High Involvement than in the Combined, and in the Combined than in the High Structure. There were significant differences ($p < .01$) between levels of leader participation across groups. Leaders participated significantly *less* in the High Involvement Condition as compared to the other two treatment conditions. While there was much less leader participation in the Combined group than in the High Structure group, the difference did not reach statistical significance.

Analysis of the audio recordings provided definitive results only on the High Involvement groups where the researcher correctly identified this condition 100 percent of the time. In contrast, the High Structure groups were correctly identified only 33 percent of the time, suggesting that there may have been more "personal"

TABLE 1. Group Observations

	DIRECTION OF DISCUSSION	
	mmbr to mmbr or grp	ldr to mmbr or grp
High Involvement	84%	16%
High Structure	7%	93%
Combined	66%	32%

discussion and member involvement in this condition than intended. While it would be expected that the Combined Condition would be the most difficult to identify due to the "mixed" nature of this condition, it was correctly identified 61 percent of the time, almost twice the rate for the High Structure Condition.

Within Condition Analysis

In the absence of significant differences between the two groups *within* each condition, the results of the two groups in each condition were combined to increase statistical power. Using the Wilcoxon Matched Pairs, we found that all comparisons showed significant shifts from pretest to posttest, except the Daily Hassles Scale, where the High Structure and Wait List Conditions did not significantly improve. Most mean differences (pre minus post), although not always statistically significant, favored the conditions utilizing group involvement, especially the Combined Condition (see Table 2).

Between Condition Analysis

We predicted that both structure and involvement were important to stress reduction. This suggests that if we combined results from all of the treatment groups to make a single treatment group (for analytical purposes only), and compared it to the Wait List group, we should see a significantly greater gain by the treatment group.

TABLE 2. Mean Differences (Pre to Post) and Significant Levels

	Hassles		SCL-90-R		POMS	
	Mean	P-Value	Mean	P-Value	Mean	P-Value
High Involve	35.9	.011	.401	.016	32.6	.033
High Structure	16.0	.098	.411	.005	32.4	.029
Combined	22.9	.012	.472	.006	38.5	.011
Waitlist	-6.9	.918	.316	.028	24.4	.033

Results on the Daily Hassles Scale supported this contention, with the treatment groups showing a significantly greater reduction of stress as compared to the Wait List group (p < .05). However, this was not confirmed by the other measures. These results are summarized on Table 3 below.

Although the subjects in the Combined Conditions did attain higher gain scores than the other treatment groups on two of the dependent measures, these differences were not statistically significant on any of the measures. These means and significance levels are shown in Table 4 below.

Lastly, we wanted to test the relative value of involvement to structure. Consequently, the Combined groups and the High Involvement groups were contrasted to the High Structure groups. The means and significance levels are shown in Table 5.

It can be seen that the treatment groups utilizing a high level of involvement showed consistently higher progress than the High Structure groups with minimal involvement, but none of these differences were even close to significant (< .05).

TABLE 3. Means of Overall Treatment Compared to the Waitlist

	Hassles*	SCL-90-R	POMS
Treatments mean	24.6	.428	34.5
Waitlist mean	-6.9	.316	24.4

*significant at <.05 (Mann-Whitney two sample test)

TABLE 4. Combined Condition Compared to the High Structure and High Involvement Conditions

	Hassles	SCL-90-R	POMS
Combined mean	22.9	.472	38.5
Struct/Involve mean	26.0	.406	32.5
P-value	.486	.178	.322

TABLE 5. High Involvement Groups versus the High Structure Groups

	Hassles	SCL-90-R	POMS
Combined/Hi Involvement mean	29.4	.437	35.6
High Structure mean	16.0	.411	32.4
P-value	.465	.651	.862

CONCLUSIONS

While the results of the participation data indicate that the manipulation of the independent variable was successful, the results of the audio tapes raise some question as to the effectiveness of creating a uniquely High Structured group. It is quite possible that sample segments were too short for accurate analysis, or that not enough segments were reviewed to attain accurate results. But it is also possible that in fact there were inadequate differences (e.g., significant involvement in the High Structured group).

When it comes to the major hypotheses, only a few of the null hypotheses could be rejected. If we used only the Hassles Scale as the dependent measure, then all treatment is significantly better than no treatment and High Involvement and the Combined Conditions are each significantly more effective in reducing stress than the control group, but the Structure Only Condition is not better than the control group. For other hypotheses with other measures, as we look at the direction of the differences of the means, they were all, at least, in the predicted direction.

While clinical observation and some of the pre-post data would lend support to the effectiveness of both structure and participant involvement, the progress of many of the members of the Wait List group offset the large gains of most of the members in the treatment groups. It is important to consider, however, that only 9 of 14 Wait List subjects returned their post-treatment measures. It is possible that Wait List subjects who made less progress or even got worse were less likely to return the measures. Earlier studies have also demonstrated positive shifts in the control group on the same measures though not to a significant degree as was the case in this study (compare with Tolman & Rose, in press).

It can be postulated that when subjects volunteered for the study, they were in crisis or at the peak of stress cycles in their lives. Whether they were in treatment or not, after ten weeks the stressors in the environment had weakened.

Another explanation of why only the Daily Hassles Scale showed significant differences between treatment and no-treatment is that the treatments may have been more effective in helping subjects deal with their daily hassles and less effective in helping them deal with other sources and symptoms of stress. The hassles inventory showed the best results on an earlier study we carried out (Tallant, Rose, & Tolman, in press). Their moods (measured by the POMS) and physical symptoms (measured by the SCL-90) may be more resistant to change through the treatments provided here.

In view of the consistently higher means for the High Involvement and Combined Conditions groups as compared to the High Structure Condition and Wait List Control Condition groups (although not statistically significant), several plausible explanations can be considered. The first conclusion may be that the lack of significance stems from low statistical power due to a low number of subjects (consequent to the large number of dropouts) for final analysis. Although not statistically significant, it should be noted that there were substantially more dropouts in the High Structure Condition and Wait List Control Condition groups where little or no group involvement occurred. Though also not statistically significant, perusal of the means reveal that the Combined Conditions group was the most successful, followed by the High Involvement Condition, and then the High Structure Condition with the Wait List Control Condition group showing the least improvement as predicted in the hypotheses.

A final problem for consideration might be that of attendance. Several of the sessions were poorly attended due to severe weather and conflicting community events. Poor attendance interfered with maintenance of high group involvement at times, especially maximum cohesion (as reflected in a member's comment, "Why isn't anyone showing up? This must not be very important to them!").

Another problem worth considering lay in the fact that posttest dependent measures for the Wait List Control Condition group and follow-up dependent measures for the treatment groups were mailed. It is conceivable that a subject may have answered the self-report measures less conscientiously while sitting in front of the television, while their child was demanding attention, or in a hurry before leaving to go shopping. Would it have made a difference if these subjects were in a professional setting with a professional emphasizing the importance of accurate answers, and with access to a professional to answer questions about the measures?

In summary, if we combine the results of this study using only the Combined Conditions group and Wait List Control Condition with previous studies (Tolman & Rose, in press, and Tallant, Rose, & Tolman, in press) it would appear that significant differences would be obtained on all the commonly used dependent measures. On this basis one can conclude that the entire package is better than nothing. When we look at involvement versus non-involvement conditions in this study we find involvement does better on at least one of the measures. When we compare the Combined Condition with the stress package only, we discover only that it is better but not significantly better. When we compare the means of the involvement measures with the structure only, we obtain the same non-significant results. In light of the heavy dropouts from the stress package only condition we have tentatively concluded that member involvement does contribute to stress reduction, but that a great deal more research is required before that assumption is adequately supported. The implication for practice until contrary findings are available, is that group involvement should not be ignored even in groups with a highly specific and structured program. And one way of incorporating that involvement is for the leader to actively involve members in all phases of the treatment process.

REFERENCES

Beck, A. T. (1976). *Cognitive therapy and emotional disorders*. New York: International Universities Press.

Bednar, R. & Kaul, T. (1985). Experiential group research. In S. Garfield & A. Bergin (Eds) *Handbook for Psychotherapy and Behavior Change* (3rd ed.). New York: John Wiley.

Bernstein, D.A. & Borkovec, T.D. (1973). *Progressive relaxation training: A manual for the helping professions*. Chicago: Research Press.

Corey, G. & Corey, M. (1982). *Groups: Process and Practice* (2nd ed.). Monterey, Calif: Brooks/Cole Publishing Co.

Derogatis, L. (1977). *SCL-90-R Manual-1*. Baltimore: Johns Hopkins University Press.

Forman, S. (1981). Stress-management training: Evaluation of effects on school psychological services. *Journal of School Psychology, 19*(3), 233-241.

Jacobsen, E. (1938). *Progressive relaxation*. Chicago: University of Chicago Press.

Kelly, J., Bradlyn, A., Dubbert, P., & St.Lawrence, J. (1982). Stress management training in medical school. *Journal of Medical Education, 57*(2), 91-99.

Kiresuk, T. & Sherman, R. (1968). Goal attainment scaling: A general method for evaluating comprehensive community mental health programs. *Community Mental Health Journal, 4*, 443-453.

Lazarus, R. (July, 1981). Little hassles can be hazardous to health. *Psychology Today*, 58-63.

Lott, A.J. & Lott, B.E. (1965). Group cohesiveness as interpersonal attraction: A review of relationships with antecedent and consequent variables. *Psychological Bulletin*, 64, 259-309.

McNair, D.M., Lorr M., & Droppelman, L.F. (1971). *Profile of mood states*. San Diego, California: Education and Industrial Testing Service.

Meichenbaum, D. (1977). *Cognitive-behavior modification*. New York: Plenum Press.

Papanek, H. (1968). Therapeutic and antitherapeutic factors in group relations. *American Journal of Psychotherapy, 23*, 396-404.

Rose, S. (1977). *Group therapy: A behavioral approach*. New York: Prentice-Hall.

Rose, S.D., Tolman, R., & Tallant, S. (1985). Group process in cognitive-behavioral therapy. *The Behavior Therapist, 8*(4), 71-75.

Schopler, J.H. & Galinsky, M.J. (1981). When groups go wrong. *Social Work, 26*, 424-430.

Tallant, S., Rose, S.D., & Tolman, S. (in press). New evidence in support of a multi-method group treatment approach for the management of stress. *Behavior Modification*.

Tisdelle, D., Hansen, D., St. Lawrence, J., Kelly, J., & Brown, C. (December, 1983). *Stress management for dental students: A multi-modal approach*. Presentation of the Association for the Advancement of Behavior Therapy, Washington, D.C.

Tolman, R. & Rose, S. D. The effectiveness of multi-modal stress management training. *Journal of Social Service Research*.

Stokes, J.P. (1983). Components of group cohesion: Intermember attraction, instrumental value, and risk taking. *Small Group Behavior, 14*, 163-173.

Yalom, I. (1985). *The theory and practice of group psychotherapy*. New York: Basic Books.

Four Studies Toward
an Empirical Foundation
for Group Therapy

John V. Flowers
Curtis D. Booarem

SUMMARY. In the first of four studies reported here, it was demonstrated that employing randomly selected client disclosures as goals in a Goal Attainment Scale method of assessing outcome in group therapy yielded positive outcome results, adding support to the use of this method of therapy outcome assessment. In the second study, employing the GAS method it was demonstrated that the percentage of positive and negative statements per minute had more impact on outcome than the number of minutes spent discussing the problem. In the third study, employing the same outcome assessment methodology, it was shown that the greater the discloser's difference in emotional induction versus subsequent reduction when discussing his or her disclosure, the greater the positive therapeutic outcome from the group. In the final study, a new method of global improvement based on the DSM III was compared with the GAS outcome. It was shown that the DSM III global assessment methodology was sensitive to the same outcome measured by the GAS method. It was also shown that the DSM III outcome assessment method was less biased by therapist expectation when the treating therapist was asked to give a best and worst case DSM III analysis of the client and the mean of these was used as the best estimate of client pathology.

The difficulty of outcome evaluation in group therapy reflects a more complex version of the problem of psychotherapy evaluation in general. Since it has been demonstrated that using specific, oper-

John V. Flowers, PhD, is affiliated with Chapman College and Curtis D. Booarem, PhD, is affiliated with the University of California, Irvine, College of Medicine.

ational outcome measures is more promising than global or personality assessment for measuring a single client's progress in therapy (Ciminero, Calhoun and Adams, 1977; Mischel, 1977), it follows that situationally specific assessment is easier to accomplish when the group focuses on a single type of problem for all members. This is probably why the greatest proportion of research in "behavioral" group therapy has been with groups of clients with homogeneous problems (Upper and Ross, 1979, 1980, 1981).

Within groups of clients with heterogeneous problems, the most common assessment methods have been of a global or personality type (Strupp and Hadley, 1977, Bergin and Lambert, 1978). When more specific measures have been employed, the most common methods use the client or the therapist(s) to rate improvement on the problem(s) being addressed. Unfortunately, this form of assessment is unsound, since reliability is unknown and validity is unassessed and compromised by response bias.

Flowers and his associates (1981, 1980a, 1980b) have employed a modified (7 instead of 5 anchored points) version of Goal Attainment Scaling (GAS), to address situationally specific client goals without relying on client or therapist ratings (Kiresuk and Sherman, 1968). In this method of assessment, prior to the group session, clients write down problem disclosures that could be made in group and the name of one rater per problem outside the therapy group who could judge the client's progress on the goal of resolving this problem. The next session the client can write down different potential problem disclosures, the same problem disclosures or a mix. If the instructions were to write 2 problem disclosures prior to each group session, in sixteen weeks duration, a client could write from 2 to 32 potential problem disclosures. Every problem actually disclosed in the therapy group becomes a client selected goal for therapy and never disclosed problems become control goals. Both types of goals are rated by external raters unaware of goal type.

In this research, it has been shown that clients improve more on disclosed than never disclosed problems, improve more on problem disclosures rated as higher than lower in intensity, and improve more on problem disclosures discussed in higher than lower cohesion sessions. While the GAS methodology employed in these studies potentially eliminates many of the problems that plague research on heterogeneous therapy groups, the goals (problem disclosures) were still client selected, and clients might have selected disclosures (therefore goals) that were going to improve because of factors other than group therapy.

The present paper reports the results of four studies. Study 1 addresses the methodological issue mentioned above to determine if client selection of disclosures biases the Goal Attainment Scaling methodology. In Study 1, instead of being client selected, the disclosures (and therefore the goals) were randomly selected for group disclosure and discussion. While this addresses the issue of selection bias, it still leaves the issues of actual group work unresolved. Even with randomly selected disclosures, any differential goal improvement could be because of the single act of disclosure rather than because of the subsequent group work done on the disclosure.

Study 2 addresses the issue of whether the amount of time spent working on a client's problem, or the frequency of positive and negative statements from other group members in such a discussion affects client improvement. While these results partially answer the question of the effect of group work on client improvement, the variable of the client's emotional response and its change because of what other group members say is also an important factor in therapeutic change.

Study 3 addresses this question by inspecting what pattern of client emotional induction and reduction in group therapy maximizes client outcome.

While the first 3 studies help verify the GAS methodology and show its utility as a group outcome assessment method, the question of whether specific goal attainment relates to overall improvement remains open. The common method of employing specific measures along with some more standard personality measure to determine if there has also been "real," "general" or "more profound" changes as well (Bergin, 1978) was not employed in these studies because it creates a theoretical polyglot and encourages the worst form of eclecticism. If the overall importance of the specific client change is to be assessed, it must be measured by devices or methods that are theoretically consistent with the nature of the group process and the specific measures employed. The final study here reports the results of an attempt to devise a general assessment device based on the DSM III to assess overall change without theoretical bias. Such a general assessment device, if verified, would augment the more specific assessment techniques generally employed in behavioral group therapy.

STUDY 1

Method

Subjects on a waiting list for group therapy at a community clinic were contacted and asked if they would be willing to participate in a group with the following specific rules:

1. The group would meet for 1 1/2 hours weekly for 16 weeks.
2. Clients would come to each group session group with two potential problem disclosures (numbered 1 and 2) written down with the name and address of a person outside the group who could rate the client's progress in resolving that problem.
3. The client agreed not to talk to any indicated rater about anything that happened in the group.
4. If the client was willing to talk during a session, one of the leaders would specify which problem to disclose (randomly chosen, 1 or 2), with the clear understanding that the other problem was not to be disclosed in that or subsequent sessions.
5. In subsequent sessions after a disclosure, the client could talk about the problem disclosed in a previous session or ask to talk about something new, which again required that two problem disclosures be written down, and that the problem discussed be chosen randomly.

Subjects

The subjects (3 males, 5 females) ranged in age from 23 to 41 (X = 27.7). The first eight people contacted from the list all agreed to participate in the group and abide by the rules of disclosure. All subjects were guaranteed participation in another therapy group without the above restrictions if they finished the experimental group. All subjects finished the treatment attending an average of 14.5 sessions each.

Therapists

The therapists were a male and female co-therapy team trained to conduct behavioral group therapy (Flowers and Schwartz, 1985).

Outcome Measures

Fifty different disclosures were made in the 16 group sessions. Two of these were on the not-to-disclose list which eliminated both those disclosures and the previously paired disclosures from research consideration; therefore, 46 random disclosures and paired 46 never disclosed problems with identified raters were employed in the outcome research. The external raters who had been identified were contacted within one week of the group's termination and were asked to rate the client's progress on the goal of resolving each disclosed and never disclosed problem on a Likert type seven-point scale in the general form:

In terms of resolving the _____ problem, in the last 4 months (Client Name) is:

1. Much worse
2. Worse
3. Somewhat worse
4. Unchanged
5. Somewhat improved
6. Improved
7. Greatly improved

Ninety of the 92 goal assessments were returned.

Results

The 45 goals which had been randomly picked to be discussed in the therapy group were rated 5.34 compared to 4.48 for goals randomly selected never to be discussed, ($t(43) = 4.33$, $p < .001$), indicating a significant client improvement even when the goal had been randomly selected to be discussed.

While Likert scales are commonly analyzed parametrically, the scale is not ratio; hence the same data were analyzed employing the Wilcoxon test to assure that the interval nature of the scale was not creating the significant difference (sum of positive pairs = 499, sum of negative pairs = 96, p < .001).

STUDY 2

Introduction

These results demonstrate that the differential improvement shown on the GAS between disclosed and never disclosed problems (goals) occurs even when the disclosures are randomly elicited. This verifies that both previous and future differential results in more normally conducted groups, wherein the client can chose what to disclose, are not merely due to the client's choice of problem disclosures and goals. What this study does not resolve is whether it is merely disclosure, or the subsequent group work that contributes to client improvement, which is the focus of Study 2.

Method

Subjects in three successive therapy groups at a community clinic volunteered and were studied for 10 one and one-half hour sessions. All subjects wrote two possible problem disclosures prior to each session with the name of a outside rater who could assess the subject's progress on the goal of resolving the disclosed problem. A subject could disclose no problem, either problem, both problems or a problem not written prior to the group in the session. If the disclosure was a problem not written prior to the group, it was written by the client after the session.

Subjects

Twenty-three subjects (10 male, 13 female) ranging in age from 19 to 44 years (x = 27.2) completed the experimental group sessions.

Therapists

The therapists were three male and female co-therapy teams trained to conduct behavioral group therapy (Flowers and Schwartz, 1985).

Outcome Measures

The first two sessions in each group were used to train the judges (graduate students in a practicum class who were not yet qualified to see clients) who collected data for the next eight sessions. Three judges independently assessed (and signaled with an arrow which could point to "on goal" or "off goal" and another arrow which pointed to a client name) whether the group was discussing a client goal (i.e., talking about a disclosure the client had made). A fourth judge recorded the time the group spent discussing the problem when two of the three judges agreed that the group was discussing a specific client's goal. A fifth and sixth judge recorded the frequency of positive and negative statements made by all group members except the client while the timer was on (Flowers, Booarem, Miller and Harris, 1974). All judges observed the group through a one-way mirror. At the end of the ten sessions, a goal list of discussed and never discussed problems was made for each client along with the outside raters the clients had indicated could rate any improvement on the goal. These external raters were then contacted to rate the clients progress on the goals.

Results

Of 2160 scheduled minutes, 2040 actually occurred. In the 2040 potential minutes, at least two judges agreed that 1666 were spent discussing a specific client's goals that were eventually rated by the external raters. Of the 74 goals that were discussed in the 24 sessions (3 groups times 8 sessions each), 72 had external raters specified and 68 ratings were returned by external raters ($x = 5.48$). The improvement on the 68 client goals correlated significantly ($r = 0.32$, $p < .001$) with the time spent discussing each goal.

In a separate analysis, the improvement on the 68 discussed and rated goals correlated significantly ($r = 0.68$, $p < .001$) with the frequency of positive plus negative statements per minute as rated by the fifth and sixth judges. The frequency of positive and negative statements per minute per goal was calculated and varied from 0.20 to 2.91. The 34 goals with the lowest positive plus negative rating per minute (intensity) was rated at an improvement rate of 4.76 compared to 6.18 for the 34 goals with the highest intensity ($t(66) =$

5.39, p < .001). An ANOVA of goal improvement by group was not significant (f(2,65) = 18) demonstrating the 3 groups were equivalent in terms of this measure of client improvement.

STUDY 3

Introduction

This study demonstrates that client improvement is not merely due to the client disclosing the problem (and the therapeutic goal) but is positively influenced by the amount of time spent in group work, and is more influenced by what might be called the "intensity" of the discussion. While the frequency of emotional statements made by other group members during a discussion correlates with the client change on what was discussed, this does not assess any differential response of the client during the group work. Instead of the "intensity" of the discussion, Study 3 assesses the effect of the client's emotionality during the discussion on outcome.

Method

In Part 1 of this study, clients in three separate therapy groups at a community clinic completed 16 one and one-half hour sessions. After the session, each member wrote down a brief version of what he or she had disclosed in the session and indicated a rater as in the previous studies. All the group members and therapists rated each disclosed problem on a seven-point Likert type scale:

1. No emotion evidenced
2. Very little emotion evidenced
3. Little emotion evidenced
4. Some emotion evidenced
5. Moderate emotion evidenced
6. Considerable emotion evidenced
7. A great deal of emotion evidenced

Each problem was rated for the highest emotion level reached by the discloser during the problem discussion and the subsequent lowest level the discloser reached prior to the end of that group session. The reason that reduction can be rated after the problem discussion is completed is that groups often return to disclosing members late in the group to assess how they are feeling. Every disclosed problem was given an emotional induction-reduction score based on the mean difference over all ratings (other clients and therapists) between the highest and lowest level of emotion rated during the problem discussion. After the termination of therapy, the outside raters were contacted for ratings in the previous study.

In Part 2, clients in a therapy group completed 16 sessions of 1 1/2 hour duration. Prior to the group session the therapists were given a random number list which instructed them to attempt to either induce or abort emotional induction of each problem as it was disclosed. In all cases where emotionality was induced, whether by therapist design or not, maximum reduction was always attempted during the session. Thus, the therapists attempted to randomly generate a set of discussed problem disclosures which had either (1) a maximum difference between the highest and subsequent lowest level of emotionality (obtained by inducing maximum emotion and subsequently reducing it to minimum levels), or (2) that had a minimum of such difference (obtained by inducing minimum emotion). The same data as above were collected. The group members were unaware of the independent variable.

Subjects

In part 1, 23 subjects (14 female and 9 male) of ages ranging from 21 to 56 years (x = 32.4) completed the 16 group sessions.

In part 2, 8 subjects (4 male and 4 female) of ages ranging from 23 to 35 (x = 25.6) completed the 16 group sessions.

Therapists

The therapists were four male and female co-therapy teams trained to conduct behavioral group therapy, (Flowers and Schwartz, 1985).

Outcome Measures

In part 1 of this study, of the 93 problem disclosures that had potential external raters, 86 ratings of goal improvement were returned by mail. These goals were given an emotional difference rating based on the mean difference between high and low emotionality ratings by the group members and leaders during that goals discussion.

In part 2, 50 separable problem disclosures were actually made to the group of which the therapists were successful in keeping the problem disclosure in the correct predetermined category of emotional induction (mean rating of 4 or below for low induction, 5 or above for high induction) in 43 cases. Seven problem disclosures were made which could not be induced (4) or could not be held to low emotional induction (3).

Results

In part 1, the 43 goals with the highest emotional induction-reduction difference were rated at 5.59 compared to 4.63 for the low emotional induction-reduction goals ($t(84) = 3.86$, $p < .001$).

In part 2, of 43 disclosed goals, 31 had external raters and 27 ratings were returned. One goal was discarded randomly to achieve the even number of goals necessary for a split half procedure, and the 13 with the highest emotional induction were given external ratings of 5.67 compared to 4.85 for the 13 with the lowest emotional induction, ($t(24) = 2.98$, $p < .01$).

STUDY 4

Introduction

While the previous three studies demonstrate the efficacy of the GAS methodology for assessing specific outcome in heterogeneous client groups, they do not demonstrate that improvement on specific therapeutic goals is related to overall client improvement. As previously stated, this is not an easily resolved assessment question. Most measures of overall improvement are both theory specific and inconsistent with the specific problem approach of behavioral group therapy. Study 4 is devoted to testing the reliability and concurrent validity of a general measure of client improvement based on the DSM III as well as testing if specific outcome results are paralleled by more generalized results. Specifically, clients in three therapy groups were assessed both on the GAS methodology and on a more general measure derived from the DSM III.

Method

Persons in three successive therapy groups at a community clinic were subjects for this study. Each subject understood that he or she would undergo four hours of individual counseling to prepare for group therapy, 24 one and one-half hour sessions of group therapy and 4 hours of individual counseling at the end of the group to determine if more group therapy was appropriate. All subjects wrote two potential problem disclosures on a card prior to each group therapy meeting as in the previous studies. At the end of the 24 sessions a goal list of discussed and never discussed problems was made for each client along with the raters the clients had indicated as potential judges who were contacted for their ratings after the termination of the therapy groups.

Subjects

Of the 27 subjects initially assigned to the three groups, 24 (9 male, 15 female) of ages ranging from 17 to 49 years (x = 29.4) completed the group and individual sessions.

Outcome Measures

Thirteen therapists (none of whom conducted the group sessions) conducted the initial four individual therapy sessions and were in fact determining the client's appropriateness for group. These therapists filled out an 80 item DSM III questionnaire on each client designed by the first author on the basis of research by McDowell (1982) and Nicolette (1982).

Fifteen therapists (none of whom had conducted the group sessions) conducted the four post-group individual sessions after group and were in fact determining the client's continued need for group therapy. All therapists filled the same 80 item DSM III questionnaire used by the pre-group therapists and were led to believe the research was a diagnostic reliability study, which was in fact going on at the clinic concurrently with the present research.

At the end of group therapy, one of the group therapists was randomly selected to fill out the same DSM III diagnostic questionnaire on each client. The other therapist in each group filled out the DSM III questionnaire twice, with the instruction to generate both the most optimistic and most pessimistic reasonable assessment of the client. Both therapists knew these data were to be used to evaluate the group's effectiveness.

The numerical answer (1 to 5) to each of the 80 questions on each client was entered into a computer program designed by the first author. This program yields a list of all DSM III diagnoses which might describe this client's problems and indicates if there is substantial or merely provisional evidence for each possible diagnosis. Thus, each of the 24 subjects received a full, computer run DSM III diagnosis before group therapy and received four such diagnoses after the group terminated.

Client goals discussed and never discussed were sent to the indicated external raters as in the previous studies.

Results

Concurrent Validity

Prior to group therapy the 24 subjects (24 computer runs) had a total of 35 DSM III diagnoses rated as substantial, or 1.46 each. After group therapy, the 24 subjects' computer run tests yielded 20 DSM III diagnoses rated as substantial, or 0.83 each, (t(23) = 4.73, p < .001). Thus, the individual independent therapists rated the subject as significantly less pathological after group therapy than before.

Since some of the diagnoses for which there was substantial evidence prior to group therapy became diagnoses for which there was provisional evidence after therapy, a second analysis was conducted in which each subject was given two pathology points for any substantial diagnosis and one point for any diagnosis for which there was some evidence. Prior to group therapy the 24 subjects had an average of 4.04 pathology points each, compared to 2.71 after group therapy (t(23) = 7.52, p < .001). Since these data are clearly not interval in nature, the same data were analyzed by a Wilcoxon test to determine if the results were created by a violation of the parametric assumptions. The results (sum of positive ranks = 268.5, sum of negative ranks = 7.5, p > .001) clearly indicated that the significant differences in pathology before and after the therapy group were not a result of a violation of parametric assumptions.

Of 127 disclosures made in group, 123 had external raters and of 106 never made, 101 had raters indicated. These were sent to the raters with a return rate of 115 disclosures made and 91 never made. Problems discussed in the group were rated with greater improvement (x = 5.57) than the goals never discussed (x = 4.65, t(204) = 5.82, p < .001). To be certain the results were not due to the non-interval aspect of the Likert scale, the same data were analyzed with a Mann-Whitney. These results were a U1 = 2910.5 and U2 = 7554.5, z = 4.56, p < .001, indicating the results were not due to the nonparametric nature of the Likert type scale rating used.

Reliability

The 24 subjects were evaluated as having 0.46 substantial diagnoses each by the group therapists who filled out a single assessment, making the most accurate diagnosis they could. This was significantly different (t(23) = 3.19, p < .001) from the evaluation given by the subsequent individual therapists (0.83). These results indicate the group therapists who had worked with the clients perceived them as significantly less pathological than the subsequent individual therapists.

The same 24 subjects were rated at means of 0.71 substantial diagnoses when this rating was derived from the average of the most optimistic and pessimistic evaluation from the other three group therapists. These results are not significantly different from the subsequent evaluations of the individual therapists (0.83). Thus, when the group leader is asked to give a range of pathology rather than give a single point estimate, the middle of this range is closer to another independent therapist's judgment of the client's present functioning than is the group leader's best estimate.

DISCUSSION

The use of client disclosures in the therapy group as goals in a Goal Attainment Scaling (GAS) assessment procedure makes the GAS method extremely easy to use in group therapy research. The use of client specified raters, unaware of what goals have and have not been therapeutically addressed, eliminates the potential biasing effect of a rater wishing the intervention to be shown effective or ineffective. The present study strongly suggests that client selection of the goal to be assessed does not affect the outcome and suggests that this method of assessment of client outcome measures primarily the effect of the therapy group on client change. While there can still be response bias, it biases both experimental and control goals, thus should not yield false positive results. This methodology provides an alternative to random assignment and control groups in the design of clinical research when the more traditional experimental control is difficult or impossible. The use of control goals rather than control groups means every subject, in a sense, is part of a simplified multiple baseline design that is not limited to clearly observable units of behavior. This is not to say that every problem of assessment has or even can be resolved by this method. Not all goals can have raters, raters are not equally reliable and the reliability is presently unknown.

Studies 2 and 3 use this methodology to inspect other aspects of group therapy. Study 2 demonstrates that both the time spent discussing the disclosure and intensity (number of positive and negative statements by other members) during the group work significantly affect the outcome. The fact that intensity is a more powerful agent than time spent is both seductive and dangerous. Simply increasing intensity could lead to group casualties just as easily as it could increase positive outcome (Lieberman, Yalom and Miles, 1973; Flowers, Booraem and Seacat, 1974). Positive change is not induced by merely increasing group session intensity, but by increasing intensity within a safe context. Specifically, intensity as measured here is made up of both positive and negative statements, not merely negative ("encounter") statements that are too prevalent in some group work.

Study 3 begins the process of investigating the variables involved in making the intensity factor work safely. Both positive and negative statements induce emotion and while emotional induction motivates change, the present study demonstrates it is the difference between emotional induction and emotional reduction that leads to positive outcome in group therapy. Clients who leave the group in a state of emotional induction without subsequent reduction may be prime candidates for change in a negative direction, i.e., casualty status. The work of Lieberman, Yalom and Miles (1973) suggests such unsafe induction may be because of an over-abundance or over intensity of negative messages in the group session. This area should clearly be addressed in future research to clearly determine what is safe and unsafe group practice.

The results of the final study replicate the results of previous work, i.e., behavioral group therapy works on the specific goals addressed in the therapy. However, this study also indicates that these results are also paralleled by the more general result of less overall pathology, strengthening the case for the significance, as well as the validity, of the results. This DSM III method of assessment is based on the assumption that pathology is reflected in diagnosis and that client improvement is indicated when a diagnosis that was a possibility is removed in the course of therapy. This assumption and therefore the assessment methodology will be weakened when the pathology is not reflected in diagnosis as in cases of family system pathology, or not necessarily reflected in individual disorders such as in low social skills. It would also be weakened in cases of confused rather than generally severe disorders; however most highly confusing disorders (e.g., Bipolar, Borderline) are also severe, nevertheless, this methodology would have to be independently verified as a general measure of improvement in such cases.

The evaluations of the group therapists under two different sets of instructions (optimistic and pessimistic) indicates that an even easier method than that employed in this study may be possible in future research. The group therapists (one per group) instructed to fill out the 80 item questionnaire to make the most accurate diagnosis, knowing that the rating was to be used to assess the group's effectiveness, evaluated the clients as less pathological than the subsequent therapists, who thought the evaluation was part of a diagnostic reliability study. This seems to be yet another example of therapist bias in the direction of self interest in outcome evaluation. On the other hand, when the other therapist in each group was asked to fill out two questionnaires on each client—one indicating the most optimistic and one indicating the most pessimistic pathological possibilities—the average of the number of DSM III diagnoses produced by these two ratings was almost identical to the subsequent evaluations of the presumably less biased individual therapists. Thus, the evaluation of global improvement may be able to be done by the therapist, provided he or she is asking the right questions—i.e., the range of pathology possible rather than the best assessment of the client's present status.

The use of the DSM III as the global measure of client improvement in group therapy (or any therapy for that matter) has a number of advantages. First, unlike other global measures, the DSM III method is not linked to a single theory of therapy. This method addresses pathology rather than personality and can be used with any other method of specific assessment. Additionally, the method employs a universal language that is understandable by therapists of any persuasion. Finally, the present method of assessment is sensitive enough to reflect changes brought about by group therapeutic intervention. At present, the DSM III outcome assessment method suffers from some of the same limitations that the DSM III itself suffers; it is limited in showing systems changes (i.e., marital or family) that are not also indicated by changes in individual pathology, and it may give falsely high pathology scores in diagnostically confusing cases.

REFERENCES

Bergin, A. E., & Lambert, M. J. (1978). The evaluation of therapeutic outcomes. In S. L. Garfield and A. E. Bergin (Eds.), *Handbook of Psychotherapy and Behavior Change: An empirical analysis*. New York: John Wiley and Sons.

Ciminero, A. R., Calhoun, K. S., & Adams, H. E. (1977). *Handbook of Behavioral Assessment*. New York: Wiley and Sons.

Flowers, J. V., Booraem, C. D., Brown, T. R., & Harris, D. (1974). An investigation of a technique for facilitating patient to patient therapeutic interactions in group therapy. *Journal of Community Psychology, 2*, 39-42.

Flowers, J. V., Booraem, C. D., & Hartman, K. A. (1981). Client improvement on higher and lower intensity problems as a function of group cohesiveness. *Psychotherapy: Theory, Research and Practice, 18*, 246-251.

Flowers, J. V., Booraem, C. D., & Seacat, G. (1974). The effect of positive and negative feedback on members' sensitivity to other members in group therapy. *Psychotherapy: Theory, Research and Practice, 11*, 346-350.

Flowers, J. V., Hartman, K. A., Mann, R. J., Kidder, S., & Booraem, C. D. (1980). The effects of group cohesion and client flexibility on therapy outcome. In D. Upper and S. M. Ross, *Behavioral Group Therapy, 1980*, Champaign, IL: Research Press.

Flowers, J. V., & Schwartz, B. (1985). Behavioral group therapy with clients with homogeneous problems. In S. M. Ross and D. Upper (Eds.), *Handbook of Behavioral Group Therapy*. New York: Plenum Press.

Flowers, J. V., Tapper, B., Kidder, S., Wein, G., & Booraem, C. D. (1980). Generalization and maintenance of client outcome in group therapy. In D. Upper and S. M. Ross (Eds.), *Behavioral Group Therapy, 1980*. Champaign, IL: Research Press.

Kiresuk, T. J., & Sherman, R. E. (1968). Goal attainment scaling: A general method for evaluating comprehensive community mental health programs. *Community Mental Health Journal*, 443-453.

Lieberman, M. A., Yalom, I. D., & Miles, M. B. (1973). *Encounter Group: First Facts*. New York: Basic Books, 1973.

Nicolette, M. (1982). Interrater reliability of the psychological scale for diagnostic classification. Unpublished Masters Thesis, North Texas State University.

McDowell, D. J. (1982). Psychiatric diagnosis: rater reliability and prediction using "psychological rating scale for diagnostic classification." Unpublished Doctoral Dissertation, North Texas State University.

Mischel, W. (1977). On the future of personality research. *American Psychologist, 32*, 246-254.

Strupp, H. H. (1978). Psychotherapy research and practice: An overview. In S. L. Garfield and A. E. Bergin (Eds.), *Handbook of Psychotherapy and Behavior Change: An empirical analysis*. New York: John Wiley and Sons.

Strupp, H. H., & Hadley, S. W. (1977). A tripartite model of mental health and therapeutic outcomes. *American Psychologist, 32*, 187-196.

Upper, D., & Ross, S. M. (1979). *Behavioral Group Therapy, 1979*. Champaign, IL: Research Press.

Upper, D., & Ross, S. M. (1980). *Behavioral Group Therapy, 1980*. Champaign, IL: Research Press.

Upper, D., & Ross, S. M. (1981). *Behavioral Group Therapy, 1981*. Champaign, IL: Research Press.